Ethical Leadership
in the Community College

Ethical Leadership in the Community College

Bridging Theory and Daily Practice

David M. Hellmich
Bluegrass Community and Technical College

EDITOR

ANKER PUBLISHING COMPANY, INC.
Bolton, Massachusetts

Ethical Leadership in the Community College
Bridging Theory and Daily Practice

ISBN 978-1-933371-22-1

Composition by Lyn Rodger, Deerfoot Studios
Cover design by Dutton & Sherman Design

Anker Publishing Company, Inc.
563 Main Street
P.O. Box 249
Bolton, MA 01740-0249 USA

www.ankerpub.com

Library of Congress Cataloging-in-Publication Data

Ethical leadership in the community college : bridging theory and daily practice / David M. Hellmich, editor.
    p. cm.
    Includes bibliographical references and index.
    ISBN-13: 978-1-933371-22-1
    1. Educational leadership—Moral and ethical aspects—United States. 2. School administrators—Professional ethics—United States. 3. School management and organization—Moral and ethical aspects—United States. I. Hellmich, David M.
    LB1779.E738 2007
    378.1'01—dc22
                                      2007005532

In memory of James C. Wattenbarger,
the father of the Florida Community College System,
a great educator and a caring person.

Table of Contents

About the Authors   *iii*

Foreword   *vii*

Preface   *x*

Part I • Foundations of Ethical Leadership

1 Virtue Theory and Leadership Theory:
   Cross-Cultural Models for Administrators and Faculty   2
   Richard B. Benner, Sr.

2 Plato's *Republic* and the Ethical Leader   16
   Gordy Wax

3 Considerations of Power, Influence, and Cultural Norms
   for the Ethical Community College Leader   23
   David M. Hellmich

4 Ethical Leadership: The Role of the President   33
   Desna L. Wallin

5 Why Presidents and Trustees Should Care About Ethics   46
   Gary W. Davis

6 Professional Ethical Identity Development and
   Community College Leadership   61
   Sharon K. Anderson, Clifford P. Harbour, Timothy Gray Davies

Part II • Daily Practice of Ethical Leadership

7 Ethical Leadership: A Faculty Obligation   78
   Beth Richardson-Mitchell

8 The Interface of Ethics and Courage in the Life
   of a Chief Academic Officer   88
   Linda Lucas

i

9 Threats to Ethical Leadership: The Hubris of Absolutism,
   the Politics of Affinity-Based Decision-Making, and the
   Development of Unethical Followers   103
   David E. Hardy

10 Leading From the Head and the Heart   122
   Susan K. Chappell

11 Transformational Leadership and Ethical Dilemmas
   in Community Colleges   131
   Sherry Stout-Stewart

12 Presidential Support for Civic Engagement and
   Leadership Education   145
   Louis S. Albert

13 A Guide to Ethical Decision-Making by Presidents and Boards   154
   Gary W. Davis

14 The Consequences of Compromised Ethical Identity
   Development in Community College Leadership   166
   Clifford P. Harbour, Sharon K. Anderson, Timothy Gray Davies

Index   *183*

About the Authors

The Editor

David M. Hellmich is vice president of learning support and academic affairs at Bluegrass Community and Technical College. Prior to this position, he served 13 years as an administrator and as an English professor at community colleges in Florida and Minnesota, and he has taught graduate courses in ethical leadership for St. Mary's University. His article "Ethical Leadership: Bridging Theory and Practice" in the *Community College Journal* was the catalyst for this book. He earned his Ph.D. in higher education administration from the University of Florida.

The Contributors

Louis S. Albert is president of Pima Community College's West Campus. He earned his master's of science in zoology and his Ph.D. in higher education from the University of Maryland–College Park. Prior to coming to Arizona in 2003, he served for five years as vice chancellor for educational services at the San Jose/Evergreen Community College District and for nearly 16 years as vice president of the American Association for Higher Education. He also has held a number of community college and university leadership and faculty positions, has served on the Board of Trustees of the International Partnership for Service-Learning and Leadership since 1990, and contributed a chapter to *Field Guide to Academic Leadership* (Jossey-Bass, 2002) titled "Presidents and Chief Academic Officers of Community Colleges."

Sharon K. Anderson is an associate professor in the School of Education at Colorado State University and is a licensed psychologist. She researches and writes in the areas of professional ethics and issues of privilege and teaches graduate courses in professional ethics. Her most recent publication is a chapter titled "Ethical Choice: An Outcome of Being, Becoming and Doing" published in *Law and Ethics in Coaching: How to Solve and*

Avoid Difficult Problems in Your Practice (Wiley, 2006). She earned her Ph.D. from the College of Education at the University of Denver.

Richard B. Benner, Sr. is assistant professor of philosophy and religion at Atlantic Cape Community College, where he teaches courses in world religions, applied ethics, and philosophy. He earned his master's degree from Florida State University and has completed postgraduate studies at the University of Pennsylvania. Prior to joining the faculty at Atlantic Cape Community College, he published articles and gave lectures to civic, educational, and business organizations on ethical leadership.

Susan K. Chappell is executive director of the Florida Community College Foundation. She earned her Ph.D. in higher education leadership from the University of Florida and came to Florida Community College from South Arkansas Community College, where she held the positions of vice president for student affairs and later executive vice president and executive director of the College Foundation. She has taught courses in college success and is the author of "Organizational Climate and Job Satisfaction: What's the Connection?," which appeared in the inaugural edition of *Visions: The FACC Journal of Applied Research.*

Timothy Gray Davies is professor and interim director of graduate programs in the School of Education at Colorado State University. He earned his Ph.D. in community college leadership from Michigan State University and joined the Colorado State faculty in 1995 to develop the doctorate program in community college leadership. Prior to joining the faculty at Colorado State, he spent 32 years serving seven different community colleges as faculty member, dean, and president. He currently is writing a book with Rick Ginsberg on the emotional, ethical, and moral elements of leadership.

Gary W. Davis joined the Illinois Community College Trustees Association in 1986 as its fourth executive director and retired from that position in 2005. He leads retreats as the principal of Board Solutions in Lincoln, Illinois, and is an adjunct professor of philosophy and the special projects coordinator at the University of Illinois at Springfield. He chairs the Council of Great Rivers Presbytery and heads the American Society of Association Executives Ethics Committee. He earned his Ph.D. in religion and ethics from the University of Iowa. His writings on ethics have appeared in publications by Jossey-Bass and the American Association of Community Colleges.

Clifford P. Harbour is associate professor and program chair of the Community College Leadership Program at Colorado State University. He earned his Ed.D. in adult and community college education from North Carolina State University and his J.D. from Ohio Northern University. Prior to joining the faculty at Colorado State University, he was dean of academic programs at Durham Technical Community College. He is licensed to practice law in Colorado.

David E. Hardy is assistant professor of higher education and director of research for the Education Policy Center at the University of Alabama. He earned his Ph.D. in higher education administration from the University of North Texas. Prior to joining the faculty at the University of Alabama, he spent 17 years as an administrator, instructor, and program developer at various community colleges and universities. He has published and presented on ethical issues confronting community college faculty, community college faculty job satisfaction, and various issues facing rural community colleges. In addition, his work with Stephen Katsinas and Vincent Lacey on a typology for community colleges was recently incorporated by the Carnegie Foundation for the Advancement of Teaching into its 2005 Carnegie Basic Classifications of Institutions of Higher Education.

Linda Lucas is director of the Master's in Education Program at Norwich University. She earned her Ph.D. in adult education from the University of Wisconsin–Madison. Prior to coming to Norwich University, she served as chief academic officer at Vermont Technical College and as an academic leader at colleges in Minnesota. She has taught courses in adult learning, educational philosophy, research methods, and the impact of technology on human and organizational behavior. Her dissertation, "The Role of Courage in Transformative Learning," won the Hosler Award at the University of Wisconsin–Madison.

Beth Richardson-Mitchell is lead instructor of communication and coordinator of the On Course Student Orientation Program at Mayland Community College. She earned her master's degree from the University of Northern Colorado. Prior to joining the faculty at Mayland Community College in 1996, she was the assistant director of The Chair Academy; she also taught English and communication classes part-time at Mesa Community College. She was recipient of The Chair Academy Excellence in Leadership Award in 1997 and has been on the advisory board for *The*

Department Chair: A Resource for Academic Administrators, an Anker publication, since 1996.

Sherry Stout-Stewart is associate dean of general education and math instructor at Piedmont Community College. She earned her Ed.D. from the University of North Carolina–Chapel Hill, where she was a two-time Smallwood Fellow. Prior to her doctoral studies, she was an adjunct math instructor in North Carolina and Hawaii. She is also a certified public school superintendent in the state of North Carolina. Her article, "Female Community College Presidents: Effective Leadership Patterns and Behaviors," was published in 2005 in the *Community College Journal of Research and Practice* (2005).

Desna L. Wallin is an associate professor in the adult education program at the University of Georgia, where her primary teaching responsibilities are in the Community and Technical College Leadership Initiative. She earned her Ed.D. in postsecondary curriculum and instruction from Illinois State University. Prior to coming to the University of Georgia, she served more than 25 years in community and technical colleges, including as president of Clinton Community College and president of Forsyth Technical Community College. Her many publications include *The CEO Contract: A Guide for Presidents and Boards* (American Association of Community Colleges, 2003) and *Adjunct Faculty in Community Colleges: An Academic Administrator's Guide to Recruiting, Supporting, and Retaining Great Teachers* (Anker, 2004).

Gordy Wax is an instructor of philosophy at Anoka-Ramsey Community College. He completed his graduate work in philosophy from the University of Minnesota and in humanities from Hamline University. In addition to teaching philosophy, he teaches Phi Theta Kappa's Leadership Development course, which explores the concepts of leadership as found in the classic literature in the humanities. He serves as an advisor for Phi Theta Kappa, whose hallmarks are fellowship, service, scholarship, and leadership.

Foreword

Leadership in our society is a privilege that enables the leader to impact both organizations and the lives of people, but it also carries many responsibilities. Perhaps the most important responsibility for anyone who is in a position of influence is to honor the public trust. While this may seem a simple and straightforward expectation, we continually read news stories about people who have violated this trust. The abuses seem to cross all vocations and walks of life, including elected officials who accept money to influence their votes, business leaders who personally benefit from backdating stock options or from falsifying financial records, military personnel and police officers who mistreat suspects and prisoners, and even scientists who misreport data.

To be sure, these stories sell newspapers. They capture the attention of readers and usually elicit an indignant reaction or a feeling of disgust. They give us something to talk about that is sure to interest other people. However, these stories diminish us all. They lead people to suspect all politicians, to distrust all leaders, and to lose faith in the fairness of our foreign policy and criminal justice system. We begin to believe in conspiracy when coincidence may be the reality. Restoring public confidence can only happen if we begin to make ethical behavior a significant value, especially for leaders in our institutions and organizations.

Community colleges, for all the good that they do for individuals and communities, exhibit the same types of lapses in ethics that we find throughout society. A search for articles in higher education and community college newspapers will yield stories about athletic scandals, sexual harassment, and misappropriation of funds. Why do these lapses continue to occur, and what can be done to strengthen the ethical foundations of our institutions? The answers to these questions can be found in *Ethical Leadership in the Community College: Bridging Theory and Daily Practice,* whose contributors present both theoretical and practical frameworks to assist community college leaders.

The definition of *leaders* should not be limited to college presidents, as leadership is disbursed throughout the organization. The president sets the tone for ethical and fair behavior, but others throughout the organization are also in positions of influence, from trustees who set policy to vice presidents, deans, directors, department chairs, and committee chairs who make important decisions every day. Ethical values are tested frequently, especially for those in such positions of influence. For that reason, it is important to think seriously about ethical values before one is faced with difficult and ambiguous dilemmas that are all too common. The contributors to this volume have done an excellent job of providing the structure for current and future leaders to examine their values and decide how they would respond to the many case scenarios.

In her chapter, Desna Wallin points out that in 2005, the board of directors of the American Association of Community Colleges (AACC), upon the recommendation of the AACC Presidents Academy Executive Committee, adopted a code of ethics for community college chief executive officers (available at www.aacc.nche.edu). Colleges should consider adopting similar ethics statements for employees and for trustees. Of course, ethics statements do not guarantee ethical behavior, but they do serve to remind leaders that ethical considerations should guide their behavior.

I have always believed that leaders should clearly state expectations for behavior. They also need to create a safe environment for employees to communicate concerns and problems without fear of retribution. Today's community colleges should be environments in which people are involved in decisions and are encouraged to take acceptable risks. Honesty and openness should be very high values for community college leaders. Judgments should be fair, dispassionate, and equitable—and in alignment with the institution's mission rather than with a conflicting self- or special interest.

As contributor Gary Davis points out, Rotary International's Four-Way Test presents a useful guide for decision-making. The story behind the Four-Way Test is instructive: Herbert Taylor was in line for the presidency of the Chicago-based Jewel Tea Company when he was asked to join the Club Aluminum Products Company to save it from bankruptcy. The challenge of rescuing the troubled company was an opportunity too appealing for him to turn down. He left his secure position at the tea company to take the presidency of the aluminum products company in 1932—the height of the Great Depression. Taylor knew he could revive the company only if he had the full commitment of his employees and only if their decisions and behavior were beyond reproach. He developed a four-question test (noted in Chapter 13) for ethical behavior that personnel were asked to memorize and that became the standard for every aspect of the company's business. Taylor credited his test for the gradual turnaround of the company. In 1943, Rotary International adopted Taylor's Four-Way Test, and it has since been translated into more than 100 languages.

I would like to think Taylor was right in his belief that businesses, institutions, organizations, and individuals guided by ethical principles will be the successful ones. If that logic is valid, the current and future community college leaders who are guided by the thoughtful information found in this book will be successful leaders.

George R. Boggs
President and CEO
American Association of Community Colleges

Preface

No institutional mission in or out of higher education is more rewarding than the mission of the community college. Few people in or out of higher education, however, face as many daily challenges in pursuing their institutional mission as do community college faculty, staff, presidents, and trustees. They are charged with educating the most diverse student body ever to enter postsecondary education's physical and virtual doors, and they are challenged to do so in the face of soaring costs and languishing budgets, ever more oversight from external agencies, and too few hours in the day to keep on top of it all.

These challenges—and many more—test the leadership skills of community college faculty, staff, presidents, and trustees. Many of these are excellent leaders who embrace such challenges as opportunities to redefine their institutions (and thereby contemporary higher education) so that they can effectively serve the ever-changing needs of their students. The very best of these faculty, staff, presidents, and trustees do so while maintaining a constant commitment to the daily practice of ethical leadership. They are the extraordinary community college leaders because they are the ethical leaders.

Ethical Leadership in the Community College: Bridging Theory and Daily Practice addresses the importance of ethical leadership and explores real-world applications so that community college leaders can develop the institutional savvy to be extraordinary ethical leaders when the avalanche of day-to-day responsibilities threatens to bury ethical intent. This collection of essays is divided into two sections: The first section provides brief theoretical foundations for ethical leadership and relates these foundations to daily practice; the second section explores in-depth daily practice for these ethical leaders.

The first section, Foundations of Ethical Leadership, begins with two essays by community college philosophy professors. In "Virtue Theory and Leadership Theory: Cross-Cultural Models for Administrators and Faculty," Richard B. Benner, Sr. examines virtue theories and theories of leadership drawn from diverse cultures in order to suggest a leadership model that contains guidelines for faculty and administrators who share in the goals and responsibilities of the community college. In "Plato's *Republic* and the Ethical Leader," Gordy Wax argues that ethical leaders are concerned about what is best for the organization; thus, they examine their decisions in light of institutional mission.

Next, in "Considerations of Power, Influence, and Cultural Norms for the Ethical Community College Leader," I explore the responsibility of faculty, administrators, and presidents for being aware of their relative positional power and for using this power to establish and enforce cultural norms that promote ethical behavior; in turn, they have a responsibility to act when made aware of cultural norms that exist beyond their primary sphere of positional power that are inconsistent with promoting ethical behavior. Desna L. Wallin follows this chapter with "Ethical Leadership: The Role of the President," in which she argues that community college presidents must set examples of integrity, fairness, openness, and consideration, because those at the top determine the tone for the entire institution. She develops this idea by exploring the meaning of ethical leadership, mythologies of ethical presidential leadership, ethical issues challenging presidents, and principles of ethical presidential leadership.

The first section ends with chapters by Gary W. Davis and by Sharon K. Anderson, Clifford P. Harbour, and Timothy Gray Davies. In "Why Presidents and Trustees Should Care About Ethics," Davis demonstrates that presidents and trustees must regularly make difficult decisions, distinguish ethical from legal obligations in making such decisions, and acknowledge that the ethical dilemmas they face do not yield to easy solutions. Anderson, Harbour, and Davies, in "Professional Ethical Identity Development and Community College Leadership," identify and explain the need for a greater commitment to professional ethical identity development in community college leadership initiatives. They conceptualize professional ethical identity development as a consequence of the successful resolution of the tension between the traditional values of the community college and the personal values developed over an individual leader's professional lifetime, and they show how professional ethical identity development may be incorporated into graduate leadership programs, statewide leadership academies, and institutional professional development sessions.

The second section, Daily Practice of Ethical Leadership, begins with chapters by Beth Richardson-Mitchell, Linda Lucas, and David E. Hardy.

In "Ethical Leadership: A Faculty Obligation," Richardson-Mitchell reflects on her vision of the community college faculty leader who communicates to students what it means to be a whole person, practices ethical leadership, and engages students in character development exercises. In "The Interface of Ethics and Courage in the Life of a Chief Academic Officer," Lucas uses paradigms of justice and caring to explore several real-life scenarios. She frames the issues and identifies questions for each scenario as well as the criteria for ethical decision-making. Hardy follows with "Threats to Ethical Leadership: The Hubris of Absolutism, the Politics of Affinity-Based Decision-Making, and the Development of Unethical Followers," in which he uses a constructed case study approach to discuss the danger inherent in absolutist ethical posturing. He concludes with a discussion of the limitations of various professional codes and with suggestions for ways that community college leaders can develop a personal ethical creed.

Next, in "Leading From the Head and the Heart," Susan K. Chappell uses concrete scenarios to explore ethical dilemmas involving conflict between what the leader knows or feels to be right and his or her sense that acting in this way might somehow put the welfare of another human being in jeopardy. Sherry Stout-Stewart follows with "Transformational Leadership and Ethical Dilemmas in Community Colleges," in which she uses several scenarios to develop her thesis that leading with commitment and having the ability to make and support decisions are the trademarks of an effective and successful leader. She also emphasizes that with the number of projected retirements in the community college system, many women who perceive themselves as transformational leaders will inevitably assume the role of CEO.

The second section ends with chapters by Louis S. Albert, Gary W. Davis, and by Clifford P. Harbour, Sharon K. Anderson, and Timothy Gray Davies. In his chapter, "Presidential Support for Civic Engagement and Leadership Education," Albert contends that community college presidents must exemplify the highest forms of professional and ethical behavior and that elected officials, community leaders, faculty, staff, and students want their presidents to be role models of ethical behavior. He also emphasizes that ethical presidents have an obligation to strive for student learning that pays attention to the student as both a future and productive member of the workforce and as an ethical and responsible citizen. Davis, in "A Guide to Ethical Decision-Making by Presidents and Boards," builds on his chapter in the first section by moving from the fact that trustees and presidents need a system for ethical decision-making to eight simple questions they can use to make ethical decisions, with each question allowing them to analyze the ethical content of their decisions. Finally, in "The Consequences of Compromised Ethical Identity Development in Community College Leadership," Harbour, Anderson, and Davies build on their first essay by using three vignettes to describe and explain strategies that reflect an inappropriate balance between personal ethics of origin and the organizational values for community college leaders. They propose an organizational process for assisting leaders in developing an integration strategy that promotes respect for personal ethics of origin and the critical values of community college education.

David M. Hellmich
September 2006

Part I

Foundations of Ethical Leadership

Chapter 1   Virtue Theory and Leadership Theory:
Cross-Cultural Models for Administrators
and Faculty
Richard B. Benner, Sr.

Chapter 2   Plato's *Republic* and the Ethical Leader
Gordy Wax

Chapter 3   Considerations of Power, Influence, and
Cultural Norms for the Ethical Community
College Leader
David M. Hellmich

Chapter 4   Ethical Leadership: The Role of the President
Desna L. Wallin

Chapter 5   Why Presidents and Trustees Should Care
About Ethics
Gary W. Davis

Chapter 6   Professional Ethical Identity Development
and Community College Leadership
*Sharon K. Anderson, Clifford P. Harbour,
Timothy Gray Davies*

1

Virtue Theory and Leadership Theory: Cross-Cultural Models for Administrators and Faculty

Richard B. Benner, Sr.

Perhaps there is no subject of philosophical inquiry that has attracted more speculation than that of virtue and virtuous people. Ancient mythologies, even those primarily examining creation, usually contain a thesis regarding the nature of virtue or morality, whether in the four successive yugas of Indian mythology, the "race of gold" in Greek mythology, the Irish first race and the first age of the world, the Sumerian *Epic of Gilgamesh,* the African story of Gassire's Lute, the Incan Viracocha myth, the emergence myth of the Navajo, the Maori creation myth of Polynesia, or the many others of the world's population. All of these speak to the issue of leadership and virtue, often without separating one concept from the other (Rosenberg, 2001).

These myths and legends form the foundations on which cultures have built their religions, philosophies, codes, and laws in an attempt to create and maintain social order. Consequently, we can find guidelines for leadership and being virtuous in the Egyptian Book of the Dead, the Code of Hammurabi, the Code of Manu, the Bible, the Qur'ān, the Upanishads, the Bhagavad Gita, or the many other surviving texts from the earliest historical times. These texts represent the best thinking of their eras on the subject of virtue, but some of these texts may also be considered timeless, with both theoretical and practical applications today.

We have, in fact, built on these traditions for thousands of years in an attempt to create a model of a virtuous person who would, in turn, become a virtuous leader. A literature review of all the possibilities and probabilities from all the traditions of the world would require many years of research and fill many volumes. But whether we trace the development of Eastern thought and application from the time of the Yellow Emperor to the present, Western thought and application from Homer to the present, or any of the traditions in between, there is much to be gained from each of these studies that may help to uncover why we are still searching for the means to understand and achieve the virtuous leader of Confucian, Platonic, or other ideal constructions.

From the mythological and early religious understandings of ethics and leadership developed many philosophical investigations and proposals for new foundations of ethical reasoning and leadership. Models have been proposed ranging from divine command theory, theory of right, rights theory, various relativisms (especially cultural relativism), utility, duty, justice, care, virtue, and the many footnotes to each of these theories, such as the "modern morality without hubris" theory proposed by James Rachels (2003).

Most of these proposals have fallen short of their mark, and many thinkers have written about the strengths and weaknesses of all of them. Perhaps the longest-lived theory, but not without controversy, is *virtue theory*. Initially alluded to in the West by Plato in his *Republic*, virtue theory is the main focus of Aristotle's *Nicomachean Ethics* and is further elucidated in his *Politics*. Virtue theory is the center of Confucian and Buddhist ethics as well as many African philosophies; it is also foundational to Hindu thought, the moral philosophy of Jesus as well as both David Hume and Friedrich Nietzsche, and postmodern feminist care ethics. With such longevity and cross-cultural significance, virtue theory appears worthy of further study as a model for leadership, as a proper function of faculty members and administrators alike.

Virtue Theory

Virtue theory, or *virtue ethics theory*, is primarily concerned with character, or the question of what kind of persons we should be. It asks questions about a person's whole life, especially, "What is the good life?" The simple answer is that the good life is the life lived virtuously—the life that displays all of the virtues consistently. The more difficult questions are, "What is virtue, what are the virtuous character traits, how are they obtained, and how are they applied?"

Usually, a virtue is identified as an admirable character trait, freely chosen and habitually acted out in a manner that benefits others as well as oneself. That such a trait is freely chosen by the actor means habitual actions based on feelings without reasoned judgment do not qualify as virtues per se. Virtues are nurtured by many years of learning and are constantly nourished by new knowledge acquired through experience. According to Aristotle, examples of virtue include courage, friendliness, gentleness, liberality, magnificence, modesty, proper pride, righteous indignation, temperance, truthfulness, and wittiness. These virtues are seen as the golden mean between the vices of deficit and excess (Aristotle, 1999).

Over a century before Aristotle, Confucius proposed a similar set of means between vices and excesses. Like Aristotle, Confucius taught that these virtues are learned over time, but he added that they become habitual through ritual. Writing at a time of political chaos in China, he believed, also like Aristotle, that virtue was essential to individual and social harmony. The foundations of the Confucian philosophy of virtue can also be found in the *Tao Te Ching* ascribed to Lao Tzu, the (possibly legendary) sage who preceded Confucius. The major difference between these two Chinese teachers is their concept of the *Tao,* or Way. Taoism, of which Lao Tzu is considered the founder, looks to nature as a whole for models of virtue, while Confucius and Aristotle looked to human nature alone. These three thinkers do share, however, the conviction that a leader must be virtuous, and that the virtuous person is a leader.

In the *Analects of Confucius,* one finds many references to the *gentleman*—the virtuous man, or leader, following the ideal way of life, or the Tao. *Te* refers to the basis for the leader's authority. It includes such attributes as generosity and humility as well as those traits that transform others and attract them to emulate the gentleman. *Jen* includes the virtues of humanity, goodness, and benevolence as well as other forms of kindness expressed as concern for all living things. These concepts are not static and may vary as one's relationship to things varies in a changing world.

As mentioned earlier, ritual plays a very important role in the habituation of virtue for Confucius. Consequently, one other term, *li,* is essential for an understanding of Confucian virtues. *Li* refers to all ceremonious behavior and the responsibilities one has by virtue of one's position in society.

It is the recognition that all persons have value and are owed respect according to their position in life and because they represent life itself.

To further specify the virtues, the *Analects* contain many of the terms of Confucius and his followers. *Benevolence* appears quite frequently, as well as *filial duty*, which is the cornerstone of a virtuous society. Also mentioned are the virtues of being respectful, trustworthy, scrupulous, loyal, sincere, cordial, kind, frugal, modest, harmonious, and cautious in speech, as well as having a sense of shame and having broad knowledge (Confucius, 1997).

The Taoist *I Ching* and the *Tao Te Ching* offer similar interpretations of virtues and the "superior man." Both of these works are much more esoteric than the *Analects,* but they are accompanied by centuries of interpretation that help the uninitiated discover the meanings behind the hexagrams and metaphors throughout the texts. Each of the 64 hexagrams of the *I Ching* refers to a virtue or the method of attaining that virtue. Among these are patience, inner strength, humility, flexibility, fidelity, sensitivity, sincerity, unselfishness, harmony, nondoing, openness, perseverance, cultivation of character, and refined illumination. Qualities or habits to be avoided are also mentioned, including desire, arbitrary exercise of power, conditioning, attachment, imbalance, concentration on externals, and mundanity. The *Tao Te Ching* discusses the virtues of humility, selflessness, detachment, moderation, kindness, truthfulness, justness, competence, openness, harmony with the Tao, and avoidance of excesses, extremes, and complacency; these are also elucidated in the many commentaries that have defined Chinese culture for centuries.

Closely allied with Taoism is the virtue theory contained in Buddhism. One need not go beyond the Eightfold Path, the way to nirvana, according to which the virtuous person is possessed of right ethical views, right resolutions, right speech, right action, right livelihood, right effort, right mindfulness, and the practice of concentration or meditation. Successful adherence to these eight steps facilitates the attainment of compassion, friendliness, clarity, and absence of desire. Subsequent commentators and schools have further articulated the Six Perfections: energy/courage, insight, generosity, patience, morality, and meditation. Mahayana Buddhism has defined the Ten Perfections, or Paramitas: generosity or liberality, morality or ethics, patience, strenuousness, meditative concentration, insight, beneficial expediency, devoted resolution, power, and transcending awareness. Also important to the Buddhist concept of virtue is one of the cardinal virtues of Buddhism—joy, which, as with Aristotle, is obtained by habit and by taking joy in all things, including relations with others.

Without reviewing every major culture, it suffices to say that each shares virtues in common with the others. Christian virtues are enumerated throughout the Bible, sharing space with the Jewish tradition in the Old Testament and adding to or restating them in the New Testament. Models of virtuous persons dating from the creation to beyond the life of Jesus abound in the Pentateuch, the Gospels, and in many other books of the Bible. The creation story in Genesis provides a starting point for a history of men of virtue such as Moses, Noah, Abraham, Job, Jesus, and Paul. Similarly, reading the Vedas and Upanishads of the Hindu tradition uncovers yet another list of virtues with more commonalities than differences with the traditions cited above. For models, one need only recall Mahatma Gandhi and his actions in both India and Africa. Many remember, and some follow, his example of nonviolent protest of injustices.

African concepts of virtue, especially south of the Sahara, are somewhat more difficult to trace, because of the oral nature of the cultures there and the influence of colonialism. Modern studies have shown that a hallmark of these cultures is a strong commitment to the welfare of the community; virtuous behavior is therefore seen as that which improves the life of the community. Truth is defined by creativity, creativity being that which makes life better. Participation in the welfare of the community is a prime virtue that involves many of the virtues previously noted. Northern African cultures, on the other hand, focus on the virtues espoused in ancient Egypt and by the contemporary Muslim community. These virtues share many of the ideas noted in Aristotle's list of virtues, especially those upheld in the Qur'ān and the life of Muhammad. This understanding includes the exemplary behavior Muhammad is said to have exercised in business and which earned him the surname of *Al-Amín,* the trustworthy.

Closely allied to sub-Saharan ideas of virtue and Taoist reliance on nature are those virtues found in the early speeches of the indigenous peoples of North America. There can be no doubt that for Native Americans, truth, trustworthiness, and respect were primary virtues. The value of courage, community, compassion, and cooperation are also apparent; prudence is mentioned, as is wisdom and right knowledge. Most of these virtues are a part of all the nations of the Americas, though their order of importance may differ between nations (Blaisdell, 2000).

This brief summary of shared virtues across a great many cultures demonstrates that of the many ethical theories available, some form of virtue theory appears to carry the broadest general acceptance. There are controversies and disagreements associated with virtue theory, but these are essentially limited to issues of how the virtues are obtained (e.g., ritual, reason, or text memorization) and the ultimate purpose of obtaining them (e.g., happiness, joy, duty, Buddha nature, or social harmony). Often the disagreements result from a failure to distinguish between descriptive and prescriptive ethics. Most virtue theories are prescriptive, stating how people ought to behave. They are meant to be transformational, taking us from what is (descriptive) to what ought to be (prescriptive). There are subtle differences across cultures as to the meaning of some of the virtues, or more precisely, the behavior that the words symbolize. Nonetheless, virtually all cultures articulate a personal transformational process, a road map moving the individual from his or her present state to a more desirable state as the person experiences life.

There are also disagreements about the nature of law and of codes and about their need and effectiveness, as well as disagreements about punishments and rewards being used to obtain virtuous behavior. A great deal of evidence suggests we do not have the definitive answers to any of these disagreements, even though our survival as a species may depend on finding better answers than we have to date.

Leadership Theory

The literature on leadership theory reads very much like that of virtue theory. Human societies appear to be in consensus that the virtuous person is a leader and that one qualifying as a leader is a virtuous person. In a modern translation of *The Counsels of Cormac*, Cormac, king of Ireland in the third century C.E., is asked the question, "What are the traditional prescriptions for a chieftain?" He responds with a list of virtues similar to those mentioned earlier; this list is later revised, producing a total of some 44 virtues (Cleary, 2004).

Sun Tzu's *The Art of War*, a guide to military leadership compiled well before the start of the Common Era, has also been a classic reference for leaders in politics and businesses. The theory contained therein was central to the post–World War II transformation of Japan into its success as a corporate culture. A reflection of Taoist culture, it stresses the concept of "doing by not doing" and "effortless effort" based on the Way (Tao). Harmony, balance, resolution, and the nature of humanity are the core of leadership based on principles and virtues (Tzu, 1988).

Whether one examines the ancient leadership texts previously mentioned, or more recent treatises such as Machiavelli's *The Prince* or Thomas Hobbes's *Leviathan,* one finds a necessary link between the virtues (or at least the appearance of virtue) and successful leadership.

In our time, theories of leadership have proliferated into the dozens. Perhaps one of the best modern overviews of leadership theory is published by the Centre for Leadership Studies at the University of Exeter in England: *A Review of Leadership Theory and Competency Frameworks* (Bolden, Gosling, Marturano, & Dennison, 2003). Bolden and his colleagues identify seven theories of leadership: great man theories, trait theories, behaviorist theories, situational leadership, contingency theory, transactional theory, and transformational theory. They also cite an evolving school of thought on dispersed leadership that changes the focus from the individual leaders and leadership in these seven theories to a collective responsibility for leadership within "leaderful" organizations.

The "great man" theory of leadership reads much like virtue theory in ethics, and is related to trait theories, which, according to Bolden et al. (2003), "draw on virtually all the adjectives in the dictionary which describe some positive or virtuous attribute, from ambition to zest for life" (p. 6). But despite the similarities between virtue theory and the great man or trait theories of leadership, virtue theory is more closely allied in its purpose with a newer theory of leadership, the transformational theory. However, before making a case for this connection, we will consider the other intervening theories and their focus.

Behaviorist theories change the focus from the character traits that leaders possess to what they actually do, based on the idea that it is easier to observe and measure behavior than it is to measure traits. Historically, this problem is implicit in Plato's dialogues (*Meno*), Confucius's *Analects*, Cormac's *Counsels*, and other ancient texts.

Bolden and his colleagues (2003) cite Douglas McGregor's 1960 thesis that "leadership strategies are influenced by a leader's assumptions about human nature" (p. 7). This thesis is explicit or implicit in all writings about virtue and leadership, especially those with a normative focus. Whether human nature is more measurable than traits is an open question.

The behavioral model of McGregor and others speaks to several views of human nature, but lacks "guidance as to what constitutes effective leadership in different circumstances" (Bolden et al., 2003, p. 8). This gave rise to the contingency or situational schools of thought about leadership. These theories of leadership focus on the situation and such factors as "the people, the task, the organization, and other environmental variables" (Bolden et al., p. 8). Bolden and his colleagues review four such models.

The great man, trait, behaviorist, and contingency or situational models attempt to discover what makes a leader of an individual who "stands out from the rest as being somehow different and 'leading' the rest of the people" (Bolden et al., 2003, p. 12). Interest in the relationship between leaders and followers is brought to the fore in theories focused on the interdependency of these two roles as opposed to just on the leader. Bolden and his colleagues review five such leading models, all of which call to mind those aspects of ancient texts such as *The Art of War,* the *Analects,* and the Bhagavad-Gita that note there is a time to lead and a time to follow. The newer transactional and transformation theories borrow extensively from the trait and the behavioral schools of leadership.

Among the five relational models is transformational leadership. According to Bolden et al. (2003), the concept of transforming leadership was first put forward by James MacGregor Burns. Citing Burn's 1978 book *Leadership*, Bolden et al. state that this leadership model is characterized by "mutual stimulation and elevation that converts followers into leaders and may convert leaders into moral agents" (Bolden et al., p. 14). As suggested, there is a relationship of mutual benefit for all parties concerned.

In the Bolden et al. (2003) review, Bernard Bass (1985) adds to this conception of transforming leadership the idea of producing social change, thus enlarging the focus to place leadership in the context of society as a whole. Further studies, such as those by Noel Tichy and Mary Anne Devanna (1986), conclude transformational leadership "is a behavioural process capable of being learned" (qtd. in Bolden et al., p. 15). In another study, Bass and Bruce Avolio (1994) state that "transformational leadership is closer to the prototype of leadership that people have in mind when they describe their ideal leader, and it is more likely to provide a role model with which subordinates want to identify" (qtd. in Bolden et al., p. 15).

Further development of transformational leadership by Stephen Covey (1992) notes that this model builds on a person's need for measuring, a need noted as far in the past as the ancient Greek philosophy of Protagoras. As with most theories of ethics, transformational leadership is concerned with purposes, long-term goals, values, and principles. This theory of leadership focuses more on executing missions and strategies without compromising human values. One of its goals is to release human potential by identifying and developing new talent. In the business domain, transformational leadership designs and redesigns jobs to make them meaningful and challenging while aligning internal structures and systems to reinforce overarching values and goals. This set of conditions is comparable to the goals and objectives of the educational system in Plato's Academy. These goals and objectives may also be found in Horace Mann's 19th-century *Common School Journal* and in many community college mission statements.

Bass and Avolio (1994) have further broken down transformational behaviors into five styles. The first, *idealized behaviors* (living one's ideals), is characterized by talking about one's ideals and the importance of a sense of purpose. This leader considers the moral and ethical consequences of decisions and talks about the importance of people trusting each other. This style of leadership champions exciting new possibilities.

Inspirational motivation style (inspiring others) is goal oriented and characterized by leaders who talk optimistically about the future and about what needs to be accomplished. They articulate a compelling vision of the future and express confidence that the goals will be achieved. They create enthusiasm among others for accomplishing the goals of the organization. This style of leadership appeals to the emotional or spirited portion of human nature.

The style of *intellectual stimulation* (stimulating others) is focused more on the rational side of human nature—critical thinking in both traditional and nontraditional or creative modes. This style encourages reexamining assumptions from various perspectives, as well as rethinking ideas that have never before been questioned. The intellectual stimulation style incorporates both the ideal of reasoning in the philosophy of Plato and Aristotle and the ideal of creativity found in African philosophy.

Individualized consideration (coaching and development) focuses on the individual and is concerned with self-development. The relationship between leader and follower is characterized by one-on-one teaching and coaching that attempts to recognize individuals' different needs, abilities, and aspirations. The leader attempts to help the individual develop his or her strengths. One is reminded of Mark Hopkins sitting on one end of a log and the student sitting on the other end.

The *idealized attributes* style (respect, trust, and faith) seeks to instill pride in others for being associated with the leader. The leader acts in ways that build the respect of others by modeling going beyond self-interest for the good of the group and making personal sacrifices for the benefit of others. This person must display a sense of power and competence. Bolden et al. (2003) note, however, inherent dangers in the measurement of competence as it relates to leadership that must be carefully addressed.

A final leadership model, *dispersed leadership,* espouses the view that everyone has a leadership role based on processes within an organization rather than defined organizational power. It makes clear distinctions between leaders and leadership, highlights the contextual nature of leadership, concentrates on the leadership process instead of individual characteristics, and is concerned with the relationships themselves (Bolden et al., 2003).

There has been an increased interest in competency theories that may play a role in future discussions about relationships, such as those between faculty and administrators. In the conclusion of "From Virtue to Competence: Changing the Principles of Public Service" (2006), Michael Macaulay and Alan Lawton note, "Competence as an *excellence* of management inevitably has the notion of virtue at its heart" (p. 709), and, "All competence, in one sense, is ethical competence" (p. 709). This understanding of competence requires further investigation, whether it is seen as a single trait or as a new theory of leadership.

Discussion

As the preceding presentation of various ethical and leadership theories shows, a key aspect of both is their transformational nature, with each having deep cultural and historical roots. Historically, the writings move from the metaphorical to the scientific, which often results in the loss of the underlying wisdom of the older texts. This movement, in itself, supports the concept of transformation as a shared reality in these interdependent fields.

As we are attempting to find models to serve as foundations for ethical relationships between community college faculty and administrators—persons intimately involved in education as both an institution and a transforming process—it appears reasonable to look to transformational

theories of leadership and ethics to provide consistency and coherency between analytically separable entities (institution, administrators, faculty)
that are dependent on one another as well as on other entities (students,
parents, staff, government, other shareholders). Given the complexity of
the institution we profess to serve—which has itself been transformed over
the years, even as it has pursued its mission of transforming students—
transformation is a key concept of which all members of the institution
must be aware at all times.

Certainly, there are areas of concern that are the special purview of
community college faculty and/or administrators. But are these concerns
reducible from the more general tenets of virtue theory and transformational leadership theory? Do they need to be addressed at the level of iso-
lated individual prohibitions such as "Do not smoke," which is contained
in at least one faculty code of ethics?

What purpose do codes of ethics serve, and how do we know? We have
had codes and laws for thousands of years, over which time they have been
constantly broken, enforced, reinterpreted, remade, or discarded. What
does the age-old breaking of and arguing over our laws and codes say about
an assumed human nature? It seems we wish to transform behavior, based
on the assumption that human nature is not inherently good, and we seem
to assume we can transform human behavior to make it meet some standard we have chosen to accept. The fact that we are free to choose is extremely important to this study, as it speaks to the issue of an assumed
human nature.

Whether we want to or not, we must consider this issue of human nature when searching for guidelines. I alluded to mission statements earlier;
these are, or ought to be, derived from our view of human nature, and they
must also be considered when searching for leadership and ethics. Mission
statements are usually very broad, because they reflect the educational institution's wide-ranging responsibilities for maintaining the delicate balance between passing on the traditions of a society while at the same time
encouraging the search for new ways to transform that society and move it
to a higher level. This new or higher level is usually based on a conception
of the "good life" that is also in a state of transformation.

Conclusion

Virtue theory provides a model of ethics that can be applied to the relationships of community college faculty and administrators. Virtue theory is accepted in varying but not incompatible forms by all major cultures and civilizations. Two areas of clear compatibility are beliefs that the acquisition of virtues is a transformational process and that the experience of knowing a human model of these virtues can be transformational as well. Modern writings on the ancient texts are beginning to identify compatibility, if not consensus, among all these ideas about virtue. Modern scholarship is also beginning to explain the more metaphorical ancient symbolisms in terms of more scientific (measurable) factors. Thus, virtue theory should not be abandoned simply because some of the traits and characteristics associated with the theory are difficult to measure. Many of these traits and characteristics are beginning to appear again in the newest forms of leadership theory—transformational theory.

"The goal of transformational leadership," asserts Stephen Covey (1992), "is to 'transform' people and organizations in a literal sense—to change them in mind and heart; enlarge vision, insight, and understanding" (p. 287). Although stated in different words, this assertion expresses the meaning behind the concerns and mission of educational institutions, including community colleges. Further, according to Covey, transformational leaders "clarify purposes; make behavior congruent with beliefs, principles, or values; and bring about changes that are permanent, self-perpetuating, and momentum building" (p. 287). Community colleges everywhere could add these concepts to their mission statements, and no one would remove them.

The educational system has the avowed purpose of being transformational. Everyone at the institution is involved in and subject to this transformational process. Behaviorally, all are expected to display virtuous characteristics; those who do not are not contributing to the purpose of the institution. The idea that we need to create a set of individualized behaviors based on a job description is both superfluous and demeaning to those who have chosen to acquire and display virtuous habits in all phases of their lives. Having virtue in one sphere of life but not in another is hypocrisy, and no model at all.

Therefore, given the coherence and continuity of virtue theory, transformational leadership theory, and the educational goals and purposes of community colleges, I advocate something I call a "normative combined theory" as a starting point for a prescriptive concept of faculty and administrator roles and relationships in community colleges, and I extend this starting point to all personnel and all relationships in educational institutions.

References

Aristotle. (1999). *Nicomachean ethics* (2nd ed., T. Irwin, Trans.). Indianapolis, IN: Hackett.

Bass, B. M. (1985). *Leadership and performance beyond expectations.* New York, NY: Free Press.

Bass, B. M., & Avolio, B. J. (1994). *Improving organizational effectiveness through transformational leadership.* Thousand Oaks, CA: Sage.

Blaisdell, B. (Ed.). (2000). *Great speeches by Native Americans.* Mineola, NY: Dover.

Bolden, R., Gosling, J., Marturano, A., & Dennison, P. (2003). *A review of leadership theory and competency frameworks.* Exeter, UK: University of Exeter, Centre for Leadership Studies.

Burns, J. M. (1978). *Leadership.* New York, NY: Harper & Row.

Cleary, T. (2004). *The counsels of Cormac: An ancient Irish guide to leadership.* New York, NY: Doubleday.

Confucius. (1997). *Analects of Confucius* (S. Leys, Trans. & Notes). New York, NY: W. W. Norton.

Covey, S. R. (1992). *Principle-centered leadership.* New York, NY: Simon & Schuster.

Macaulay, M., & Lawton, A. (2006, September/October). From virtue to competence: Changing the principles of public service. *Public Administration Review, 66*(5), 702–710.

McGregor, D. (1960). *The human side of enterprise.* New York, NY: McGraw-Hill.

Rachels, J. (2003). *The elements of moral philosophy* (4th ed.). New York, NY: McGraw-Hill.

Rosenberg, D. (2001). *World mythology: An anthology of great myths and epics* (3rd ed.). New York, NY: McGraw-Hill.

Tichy, N. M., & Devanna, M. A. (1986). *The transformational leader.* New York, NY: Wiley.

Tzu, S. (1988). *The art of war* (T. Cleary, Trans.). Boston, MA: Shambhala.

2

Plato's *Republic* and the Ethical Leader

Gordy Wax

In November of 2002, I had the privilege of listening to Frances Hesselbein, former CEO of the Girl Scouts of the USA, speak about leadership. I was inspired and bought her book, *Hesselbein on Leadership*. In this book, Hesselbein argues that effective leadership is mission-focused, values-based, and demographics-driven. Her thoughts on leadership have affected how I teach my leadership classes and how I work at developing leadership with students in Phi Theta Kappa, the International Honor Society of Two-Year Colleges.

Hesselbein argues empirically that being mission-focused, values-based, and demographics-driven is essential for effective leadership. My concern in this chapter, as a professor of philosophy, is to provide a theoretical argument, based on Plato's *Republic,* that being values-based (i.e., having ethical principles) is essential for being an effective leader.

Justice, Guardians, and Rulers

In the *Republic*, the protagonist Socrates becomes engaged in a discussion about the nature of justice. In Book I, Socrates, Cephalus, and Polemarchus try to define justice. Not until Thrasymachus enters the discussion (Plato, 1992, p. 338c), asserting that justice is the advantage of the stronger over the weaker, is the notion of justice tied to a relationship between at least two people and, hence, potentially tied to leadership.

Thrasymachus argues that the rules of justice are not ethical principles but rather are methods rulers use to manipulate others for their own benefit. Socrates (pp. 341c–342c), on the other hand, argues through the analogies of the physician, the ship's captain, and the horse breeder that rulers, rather than seeking their own advantage, seek the advantage of those that they rule. Book I ends (p. 354b) with Socrates disappointed because he has yet to discover fully the nature of justice.

This opening dialogue sets up the rest of the discussion in the *Republic*. At the beginning of Book II (pp. 357b–361d), Glaucon lays down the gauntlet for Socrates and challenges him, not only to find the nature of justice, but also to show how and why it is better to be just than unjust. This leads Socrates on his journey in search of justice in a theoretical city, after which he applies what he finds in this city to the human soul.

Relevant for our purposes are the values of the leaders of the various types of constitution that Socrates discusses and why the most effective leaders of a city (or any organization) are those with the best values: love of wisdom and, specifically, wisdom concerning the good, according to Socrates.

In Book II of the *Republic*, Socrates begins to construct the theoretical city. He describes a Wealthy City (pp. 373b–383c), since his friends insist on having luxuries. In creating such a city, Socrates realizes that the city must be further enlarged by an entire army (p. 373c). The result is a city with stratified social classes, including the Guardians and the regular citizens, to whom Socrates will later refer as the Moneymakers. Unless the citizens are to be enslaved by the Guardians, Socrates describes the characteristics the Guardians must possess: They must be spirited and philosophical by nature (p. 375e); they must use love and knowledge as the bases for judging (p. 376b); they must be lovers of learning (p. 376c); and they must be moderate (p. 389e). Hence, Socrates has purified the luxurious city by making it moderate via such Guardians.

Now, of course, the question arises as to who will be the best rulers of this city. In Book III, Socrates answers this question by describing the attributes of Rulers: They must be older than the general population (p. 412c) and the best ones at guarding the city, and they must think that what is best for the city is also best for them (p. 412d) so that they will not have conflicts of interest. In other words, the Rulers must value the good of the city.

To avoid any conflict of interest, Rulers should not possess any private property beyond what is necessary, nor should they have a house or store-room that is not open to all. They should receive moderate sustenance through taxation and live like soldiers in a camp (p. 416d). The Rulers' lives in the city should be such that the only good for them is what is good for the city.

Glaucon raises the objection that the Rulers, being denied wealth and other personal gratifications, will not be very happy in this city. Nevertheless, Socrates responds, "Our goal is not to make any one group happy, but to make the city as a whole as happy as possible" (p. 420b). Furthermore, because these Rulers value what is best for the city, they will be happy if they have established good leadership over it. Socrates argues that this city will be "one city" and will be at peace with itself, because the citizens will follow the Rulers' decisions, knowing that these decisions will always be in the best interest of the city as a whole.

The Ethical Leader

Drawing on what Socrates has said about the Rulers of a city, it is possible to make some inferences about leadership in general. Good leadership is ethical leadership; it values the good of the group over the good of the individual. Specifically, leaders need to be mission-focused, meaning leaders must believe that the purpose of the group or organization is connected to their own values such that the success of the organization's mission is intimately connected to their own happiness. Thus, they must think that what is best for the group or organization is also best for them. Such leaders, for Socrates, are true philosophers.

Socrates argues in Book VI (pp. 485–499) that ethical leaders must be without falsehood, meaning they must not feign a primary desire for the good of the organization, but must truly believe that their own good is intimately connected to the good of the whole. They must not be lovers of money, because such people will always have an internal conflict of interest between the organization and themselves. Leaders must not be petty, because pettiness is at the root of conflicts. They must manage conflicts within the organization by focusing everyone's attention on the mission, and they themselves are not afraid of conflict, nor even of death.

While most of today's organizational leaders will not be faced with life-or-death situations, they will frequently be faced with decisions that involve conflict, possibly even resulting in personal psychological and emotional pain. True leaders will value the organization's mission enough to endure conflict and even pain because of the value they place on the mission.

Finally, Socrates argues that ethical leaders must be reliable and just. Others depend on them because of their commitment to the mission, and the leaders will be just to the extent that they mete out rewards and punishments based solely on merit.

Socrates argues in Book VI (pp. 505–511) that true leaders will be driven by the idea of the Good. They will be driven by their understanding that the mission of their organization is good and, therefore, worthy of pursuing—not just for the good things that will be derived from it, but also for the virtue of the mission itself. They will lead and inspire others to the same sort of focus on the mission by examining the good that is to be found in the mission. Socrates uses the Allegory of the Cave in Book VII to drive home this point.

Socrates describes a scenario in which people live like prisoners in a cave. All they know are the shadows projected on the wall from the fire that is behind them, and they believe these shadows depict reality. Then, a prisoner is released and led out of the cave. At first, this prisoner is blinded by the sunlight; he is dazzled and confused. After a long time, he adjusts and comes to see the world as it truly is. When he returns to the cave, the other prisoners believe he has been "ruined" by the sunlight such that he can no longer function in the cave. No one else wants to be released, for fear that he or she too will be ruined. And yet, who is better off? Socrates argues it is the person who has seen the light and recognizes that the shadows in the cave are merely illusions.

The prisoners in the cave are similar to members of an organization who are part of that organization primarily for reasons like pay and other shadows that might be projected before them to make them contribute to the mission. Organizational leaders need to be like the released prisoner who has seen the light; they need to show the others that the value of the organization's mission is worthy as an end in itself. They exhibit such leadership by releasing others from their psychological chains and turning them in the direction of the light; they do this by focusing on the value of the mission, the good of the mission. By so doing, leaders empower others in the organization and make the organization more effective.

This type of organizational leadership is driven by values related to the good of the mission; Socrates calls this type of leadership an *aristocracy,* from the Greek word meaning simply, "rule by the best" (i.e., rule by those whose values reflect what is best for the city or organization). This may be compared to four other types of leadership that Plato has Socrates discuss in the *Republic*.

Alternatives to Ethical Leadership_____

The second type of leadership Socrates discusses is that found in the Timocratic constitution (pp. 546–550c). In this constitution, the leaders value Victory and Honor above everything else. Such leaders can also be fairly effective, because, in order to achieve victory and honor, leaders need to accomplish their mission. However, these leaders do have their drawbacks, as pettiness can creep into an organization if cooperation is replaced by competition as to who gets the credit (the honor) for accomplishing the mission. Falsehood also rears its ugly head; since honor is more valuable than the good of the group, individuals will lie to obtain victory and the appearance of honor; this, of course, can fragment an organization and ruin the integrity of leaders. Moreover, if honor replaces mission as that which has the highest value, then energy and resources will be focused toward attaining honor. If the mission is not achieved, then the blame game begins, because those who value honor disdain blame, and energy is then focused on ascribing blame to others.

Next, Socrates describes the Oligarchic constitution (pp. 550d–555b). In this type of leadership ("rule by the few"), money is valued above all other things. The rich rule, and they value money at the expense of virtue (the organization's mission). The city (or organization) becomes divided between the rich and the poor. If leadership is driven by money, then the organization becomes entirely fragmented—why should anyone care about the mission of the organization if the leadership does not? Everyone is driven by money. Cooperation is replaced entirely by competition. Leaders and followers struggle with the conflict between what is in the interest of the organization and what is in their own interest; pettiness and falsehood are prevalent, and fear of pain and death discourages anyone from taking a risk that might help the organization succeed in its mission. This type of leader will tend to lose all integrity within an organization.

Socrates then discusses the Democratic constitution (pp. 555b–562). He argues that this type of leadership ("rule by the people") comes about when the poor are victorious. All people have an equal share in ruling; they are free, and everyone does what he or she wants. There is a great variety; this is rule by committee. Everyone brings his or her own values to the organization, and each value is the equal of any of the others. The good leaders (those who know what is best for the organization) are not taken any more seriously than anyone else. The mission of the organization is taken over by the various missions of the individuals. There is neither order nor necessity in this type of leadership, and nothing gets done. While individuals feel empowered because of their freedom, they have lost their sense of purpose and identity with the organization.

What could possibly be worse? Socrates describes Tyranny (pp. 562–571), arguing that this leadership style arises from a democracy because of its ineffectiveness. Nothing can get done because the opposite positions cancel each other out. People need someone to lead; thus, they choose a leader. But this new leader is driven by his or her individual values and mission, not the mission of the organization. Since things get done, people within the organization appear to be happy, but it is only because they have completely lost sight of the organization's mission. They are like gerbils in a cage. They spin their wheels for eight hours a day, yet they have accomplished nothing meaningful. They are busy but unfulfilled. They are disgruntled. From the outside, others who are interested in the organization's mission stay clear, so it becomes nearly impossible to recruit new members who may help right the organization. Socrates argues that while these types of leaders may seem happy, they live without friends, they are untrustworthy, and they are enslaved and afraid. In a nutshell, they are wretched. They are the worst possible leaders. While these individuals may seem to wield a vast amount of power, the selfishness of their personal values has rendered them completely ineffective as leaders.

None of these other leadership styles is as effective as the ethical leader, the one whose leadership is based on the values of the mission and what is best for the organization. There is nothing that these other types of leaders can do to make their organizations more effective if their values are not based on the mission of the organization. If Plato and Hesselbein are right, all of the other aspects of leadership (setting goals, making decisions, empowering and delegating, building teams, managing conflict, and interacting with other organizations) are driven by the values of an organization's leadership. Hence, true leadership cannot exist without ethics being an essential element.

Solutions

There is no easy fix to the problem of becoming ethical leaders; there is nothing that can simply be done and then checked off some list. It is not a matter of simply taking a three-credit course on ethics, attending a day's seminar, or reading an ethical leadership essay. Rather, ethics are brought to leadership roles. They are not a matter of what to do but are what people choose to be. If people want others to think they are ethical leaders, they must not simply appear to be ethical, since their true values will eventually become apparent; they must really *be* ethical leaders.

Ethical leaders, as Plato has described in the *Republic,* are always concerned about what is best for the organization and are always searching for the knowledge of what is best. Ethical leaders examine and question their own actions and decisions based on their organization's mission. I have a copy of my college's mission posted on my office door, and I read it every morning when I arrive on campus. Ethical leaders examine and question even their organization's mission, and they seek to adjust the mission accordingly.

If leaders are of this nature, then all their actions and decisions will be in harmony with their values. As Plato argues through Socrates (and as philosophy professors are keen to emphasize), the best leaders, the ethical leaders, must be philosophical in nature.

References

Hesselbein, F. (2002). *Hesselbein on leadership.* San Francisco, CA: Jossey-Bass.

Plato. (1992). *Republic* (2nd ed., G. M. A. Grube, Trans.). Indianapolis, IN: Hackett.

3

Considerations of Power, Influence, and Cultural Norms for the Ethical Community College Leader

David M. Hellmich

A community college, like any organization, consists of a complex matrix of cultural norms. Many of these norms are obvious to the casual observer taking an afternoon stroll across campus or surfing the college's web pages. They are evident in how instructors greet students at the beginning of class, in how staff respond to simple questions from strangers, and in what information is highlighted, buried, or omitted from college publications. When these norms principally work in concert to advance the mission and vision of the college, a successful organization emerges. When these norms also principally promote ethical behavior, a functional as well as successful organization emerges—one that not only achieves its mission and approaches its vision, but that is also a rewarding place to be a student, employee, and visitor and that is a model for other community colleges nationally.

All community college faculty and staff possess varying degrees of power to create, preserve, and alter the cultural norms within the organization. With this power, faculty determine many of the cultural norms in their classrooms and in their departments; administrators determine many of the cultural norms in the segments of the college for which they have responsibility; and the president determines many of the cultural norms for the institution at large. Faculty, administrators, and the president thus have a responsibility to be aware of their relative power and influence and to use it to establish and enforce cultural norms that promote ethical behavior. They also have a responsibility to act when made aware of the existence of cultural norms inconsistent with promoting ethical behavior.

Considerations of Power and Influence _____

According to political scientist Elias Berg (1975), having *power* means being "able to affect deliberately (positively or negatively) other people's aims" (p. 219), while having *influence* means being "able to *deliberately enlist others in support of one's own aims*" (p. 220). Power is typically tied to the formal structures of organizations, whereas influence is tied to informal social structures just as often as to formal structures. A person in a position of power may have a great deal of influence or virtually no influence at all; likewise, a person in a position of limited power may have limited influence or a great deal of influence: "We have seen that power can produce influence and that influence can produce power. We have also seen that the two can be opposed in the same social relationship" (Willer, Lovaglia, & Markovsky, 1997, p. 595).

Within these considerations, faculty, administrators, and presidents all possess power. Faculty have the power to teach their classes as they think best. While workload realities involving class size and the number of course preparations, and institutional practices involving textbook selection and instructional technology support, for example, can have profound impact on an instructor's zeal and effectiveness, what happens in the classroom (both face-to-face and virtual) is almost entirely within the purview of the faculty member. Faculty also typically have structural power at the department level to determine departmental practices, and they have structural power at division and college-wide levels through faculty representatives to help determine academic and institutional practices.

Administrators have the power to manage and lead the segments of the college for which they have responsibility. Institutional policies and procedures, federal and state mandates, and faculty and staff contracts are examples of bureaucratic realities that can make managing difficult on good days and dreadful on less-than-good days, and which can impede all inclination to take the initiative to lead organizational change. Nonetheless, administrators have the power to affect the extent to which these bureaucratic realities are acknowledged and whether personnel are expected to have a student-centered and customer-service-oriented attitude. Administrators also have the structural power within their areas of responsibility, and typically some influence beyond these areas, to initiate organizational change.

Presidents have the power to manage and lead the college at large. In addition to the bureaucratic realities encountered by their administrators, presidents must deal with a myriad of challenges involving boards of trustees, regional accrediting bodies, and a host of influential persons and groups external to the college. Increasingly, these challenges involve delicate discussions with purse-string-holding legislators who come into office pronouncing that higher education is inefficiently managed and who are quick to quote (and misquote) overly simplistic accountability data in support of their stated goal of moving colleges toward operating with businesslike effectiveness. Increasingly, these challenges also involve obsequious discussions with potential donors whose philanthropy is more critical than ever to realizing institutional initiatives. While many such donors are honorable people with an honest love for the institution, some are transient supporters with agendas not aligned with the college's mission, vision, and values. While facing such challenges, presidents have the power to affect cultural norms at all levels of the institution, and most faculty, staff, administrators, and external leaders are quick to judge every action and nonaction of the president as a validation or betrayal of those institutional cultural norms they hold most dear.

Faculty, administrators, and presidents may or may not possess the levels of influence typically associated with their positions. Every community college is privileged to have faculty and administrators whose influence is far-reaching. People who monitor the subtle ebb and flow of organizational culture know who the people with influence are. They know the faculty and the administrators who speak with the best interests of the students in mind, who calmly sift through faculty-versus-administration demagoguery and speak their truth no matter which side this truth seems to support, and who are the first people community leaders call to find out what is "really going on" at the college. They know the faculty who are sage leaders within their disciplines; they know the administrators who can navigate institutional bureaucracy to get things done, even if the issue of the moment is as trivial as getting inter-campus travel reimbursement.

Likewise, every community college is cursed with faculty and administrators whose influence is far-reaching but directed toward the dark side. Only people who make concerted efforts to be oblivious to organizational happenings do not know these faculty and administrators. These are the ones, for example, who actively build coalitions of like-minded people so they can impose professionally egoistic views throughout the organization, who loudly criticize nearly everything new and actively export their criticisms throughout the organization with a healthy dose of conspiracy theory added for effect, and who have mastered the rules of their turf and relish when they can lord these rules over those with less power and influence.

Every community college is also hampered by faculty and administrators whose influence does not extend as far as it should. These are the faculty and administrators, for example, who have abrogated the influence that accompanies their positions by retiring on the job years ago, by not valuing the mission of the public community college, or by not having sufficient expertise in their areas to command the respect of students and colleagues. At best, they are the "status quo oriented persons and groups [that] influence those community values . . . which tend to limit the scope of actual decision-making to 'safe' issues" (Bachrach & Baratz, 1962, p. 952). More often, they are the infamous deadwood that educational critiques so quickly point to as institutionalized examples of deficient accountability and substandard effectiveness.

On the presidential level, many community colleges are fortunate to have presidents whose influence is greater than their structural power; others are less fortunate to have presidents whose influence is a mere shadow of what it needs to be. The former is represented by the self-assured president who is respected by nearly everyone at the college and in the community, who has created a dynamic team and trusts team members to do their jobs well, and who has actively worked to develop an organizational culture representing the best of the school's mission, vision, and values; the latter is represented by the insecure president who is known by many but respected by few, who has created a dysfunctional team by managing either too little or too much, and who has actively worked to develop an organizational culture that reflects his or her personality more than the college's mission, vision, and values. The influence of the former president comes partly from his or her understanding that because "power is energy, it needs to flow through organizations; it cannot be bounded or designated to certain functions or levels" (Wheatley, 1999,

p. 40). The lack of influence of the latter president largely comes from not having such an understanding.

Considerations of Cultural Norms

Faculty and administrators as a group, consisting of individuals with quite varied degrees of power and influence, play vital roles in forming the culture of a community college, as does the president, whose power and influence typically shape the college's culture more than any other single person. James Wattenbarger, the founder of the Florida Community College System, was fond of telling people that all they had to do to get insight into the culture of a community college was to call the switchboard and talk briefly with the receptionist. Tone of voice, availability of information, general customer-service attitude, and overall professionalism quickly inform the caller about what is valued at that institution.

Every faculty member, every administrator, and the president bring their unique personal cultures to the organization; every academic and administrative department has its own culture, and every relationship of any consequence develops norms of interaction. These unique cultures and these interactional norms come together to create the overall culture of the community college. Those persons with the greatest power and influence have the greatest influence in determining this overall culture and its norms.

Cultural norms at the individual level, at the academic and administrative department level, and at the college-wide level are "behaviours, dispositions, knowledge, and habits [that have been] internalized through socialization" (Ecclestone, 2004, p. 31). These norms accumulate varying degrees of *cultural capital,* a sociological term that emphasizes the value that the culture places on them. The greater the cultural capital associated with a particular cultural norm, the more likely this norm will be retained, and, as important, the more likely it will be internalized as a norm by new people coming into the cultural environment of the department and college.

Thus, not only is it important for all faculty, administrators, and the president—especially those with the greatest organizational power and influence—to be aware of their personal cultural norms and to be aware of their contribution to the creation of department and college-wide cultural norms, but it is also imperative that this awareness leads purposefully to norms with solid ethical foundations.

Considerations of Ethics_____

In working with practitioners in community colleges and in local community leadership development programs, I have found three texts to be especially clear and effective for exploring the importance of ethical behavior.

The first is John H. Zenger and Joseph Folkman's *The Extraordinary Leader* (2002). This is a research-based and business-focused book that emphasizes the importance of ethical behavior. The authors squarely claim that without possessing ethics people "will absolutely not be perceived as great leaders" (p. 57), and they argue that being a person of sound character is the single most important trait in becoming a successful leader. They go on to argue that the most accomplished leaders have a profound impact on the organization's overall success. This argument, therefore, is an effective way to begin the discussion of ethical behavior, because, while being an ethical professional should be a worthy goal by itself, Zenger and Folkman articulate the bottom-line professional and organizational impact of ethical behavior.

The next two texts, which are excellent in clarifying the nature of ethical acts, are Robert Kane's *Through the Moral Maze* (1996) and the Dalai Lama's *Ethics for the New Millennium* (1999). Kane notes in his text that the core of ethical behavior is expressed in "The Golden Rule" (do unto others as you would have them do to you), which is articulated in all major world religions, and he presents an extension of Immanuel Kant's *categorical imperative* as a more precise statement of ethical behavior: Every person has intrinsic worth and, as such, has a right to be treated whenever possible as an end and not as a means to someone else's ends, and that an act is ethical if it adheres to this imperative. Kane further emphasizes that everyone has the responsibility to stop behavior that is not ethical, using as little force as possible.

Kane (1996) applies this imperative through the metaphor of the ethical sphere. This sphere exists when everyone is treated as an end, that is, when no one is consciously using someone else just to get what he or she wants—think of a faculty and staff committee meeting in which everyone is engaged in the topic and is respectful of the contribution of the other committee members. If the ethical sphere is broken by an obviously guilty party who is using one or more people as a means to his or her own end—consider the committee member shirking committee responsibilities and leaving the work to others—people have a responsibility to restore the ethical sphere with the minimum necessary force. If the ethical sphere is broken but no guilty party exists—imagine the college laying off faculty and staff in a low-enrollment program in order to shift resources into a growing or new program—people continue to have the responsibility to restore the ethical sphere. In this situation, Kane acknowledges, "someone will be treated as a means, but we must strive to decide who it will be by the fairest possible procedure" (p. 39). Assuming students and the community will best be served by shifting faculty and staff resources from one program to another, Kane would argue that the college in this last example ethically may dismiss the faculty and staff.

Like Kane, the Dalai Lama (1999) ties ethical behavior to how one treats other people and emphasizes the sense of responsibility that goes with acting ethically:

> To develop a sense of universal responsibility—of the universal dimension of our every act and of the equal right of all others to happiness and not to suffer—is to develop an attitude of mind whereby when we see an opportunity to benefit others, we will take it in preference to merely looking after our own narrow interests. (pp. 162–163)

Such universal responsibility is inconsistent with the parochial attitude of some faculty, who see their professional responsibilities as being limited to their classes, and some staff, who see their professional responsibilities as being limited to their department; it also belies the attitude that a person is not responsible for addressing the unethical actions of others. The Dalai Lama would argue that everyone within the community college is connected through the universal responsibility to assist one another and through the reality that even acts intended to have impact only in a classroom or only in an office actually have much broader impact within the college. Tying the Dalai Lama's view of ethical behavior to Kane's provides a multicultural perspective and reinforces the need to look beyond ourselves and to act when encountering unethical events.

Together, Kane and the Dalai Lama present a lucid and sophisticated analysis of universally just behavior. They provide clear definitions of ethical behavior and clear expectations for responding to unethical acts. Add to this analysis Zenger and Folkman's (2002) empirical evidence that ethical behavior increases one's effectiveness as a leader—and thus one's power and influence—and practitioners like community college faculty, administrators, and presidents have a clear rationale for acting ethically and a solid foundation of ethical understanding that includes their responsibility to act when unethical actions occur.

The Responsibility to Act

Daily ethical behavior is the cultural norm for most faculty, administrators, and presidents at most community colleges. Routinely, faculty bring creativity and passion to their teaching assignments and dutifully engage in departmental and college business; administrators approach their responsibilities with conviction and seek to improve their departments and the college; and presidents shoulder the weight of college-wide duties with great concern and dignity.

At the same time, however, less-than-ethical behavior, like the following, on the part of faculty, administrators, and presidents occurs on occasion at most, if not at all, community colleges:

- A faculty member uses the classroom to advance his or her political and personal agenda, thereby preventing students from mastering department-approved curriculum and causing the college to stumble in achieving its mission related to student achievement.

- A dean gives a poor reference to an excellent director, thereby sabotaging her efforts to land a promotion and causing the college to fail in its vision of being supportive of faculty and staff professional development.

- A president quietly buries a faculty-driven curriculum initiative after it has completed the curriculum review process because he sees the initiative as inconsistent with his political views and the views of key external constituents, thereby eroding faculty trust in administrative support for the agreed-upon curriculum review process and causing the college to fall short in its mission of providing students with innovative curricula.

- A vice president views deans and directors essentially as servants to be publicly rebuked, thereby resulting in low employee morale and causing the college to fall short in realizing its vision of being a true learning institution.

- A faculty grievance representative sends an all-faculty email demanding a grievance a week even when there is nothing to grieve, thereby straining the already tenuous relationship with the administration and causing the college to falter in its vision of a healthy work environment.

The behavior in each of these examples is unethical because the faculty member, administrator, or president is using others as a means to his or her ends and does not treat others as intrinsically worthy and with a right to happiness. In addition, the behavior is contrary to the highest purposes of the college as expressed in the mission and vision; in some cases, the behavior may also violate institutional policy or procedure.

When such behavior occurs, it is easier to dismiss the behavior than to address it. It is easy to rationalize that the behavior affects an area of the college other than one's own, that it is an anomaly in an otherwise ethical college culture, or that it is essentially irrelevant since everyone "expects this type of behavior" from this person. It is easy to play the role of Sergeant Schultz from *Hogan's Heroes* ("I see nothing! Nothing!") for fear that addressing the unethical behavior, especially when people with power and influence are involved, will result in direct or indirect retaliation.

While weighing the costs and the benefits of an action before taking it is prudent, one must include in this cost/benefit calculation the cost of doing nothing, since doing nothing to stop unethical behavior, according to Kane (1996) and the Dalai Lama (1999), is in itself unethical. Every member of the community college—every faculty member, every administrator, and the president—has a professional obligation to acknowledge unethical behavior and to decide, while using his or her own cost/benefit calculation, the best means of addressing this behavior. The more power and influence a person has within the culture, moreover, the more responsibility this person has to see that such unethical behavior does not become a cultural norm. In so doing, this person will be acting ethically to establish and enforce cultural norms consistent with ethical behavior.

References

Bachrach, P., & Baratz, M. S. (1962, December). Two faces of power. *American Political Science Review, 56*(4), 947–952.

Berg, E. (1975, May). A note on power and influence. *Political Theory, 3*(2), 216–224.

Ecclestone, K. (2004, March). Learning in a comfort zone: Cultural and social capital inside an outcome-based assessment regime. *Assessment in Education: Principles, Policy, and Practice, 11*(1), 29–47.

Kane, R. (1996). *Through the moral maze: Searching for absolute values in a pluralistic world.* New York, NY: North Castle.

Lama, D. (1999). *Ethics for the new millennium.* New York, NY: Riverhead Books.

Wheatley, M. J. (1999). *Leadership and the new science: Discovering order in a chaotic world* (2nd ed.). San Francisco, CA: Berrett-Koehler.

Willer, D., Lovaglia, M. J., & Markovsky, B. (1997, December). Power and influence: A theoretical bridge. *Social Forces, 76*(2), 571–603.

Zenger, J. H., & Folkman, J. (2002). *The extraordinary leader: Turning good managers into great leaders.* New York, NY: McGraw-Hill.

4

Ethical Leadership:
The Role of the President

Desna L. Wallin

At any level, in any sector in society, a public leader automatically takes on the responsibility of moral or ethical leadership.
—George Vaughan

In any decision-making situation, ethical issues are either implicitly or explicitly involved. The choices that leaders make and how they respond in a given circumstance are informed and directed by their ethics.
—Peter Northouse

Because those at the top set the tone for the entire institution, it is critical that the community college president set an example of integrity, fairness, openness, and consideration. It is not sufficient for the president to be a strong, well-connected, and intelligent leader; the successful president must also be an ethical leader.

Just what does it mean to be an ethical leader? How does the study of ethics relate to the study of leadership? This chapter will discuss definitions of ethics, particularly as applied to the community college president; ethical perspectives as applied to community college leadership; common mythologies surrounding ethical leadership; challenges of ethical leadership in the community college; and principles of ethical presidential leadership.

Definitions_____

Ethics, like leadership, is defined in many ways. It is most often linked to the field of philosophy, along with other areas such as logic, metaphysics, and aesthetics. From a Western perspective, ethical theory dates back to Plato and Aristotle. The word *ethics* has its roots in the Greek word *ethos,* which relates to customs, conduct, or character. It is concerned with the values and morals that a particular society finds appropriate. John Dewey (1902) saw ethics as the science that deals with conduct regarding right and wrong, good and bad.

Ethics is also concerned with "the virtuousness of individuals and their motives" (Northouse, 2004, p. 302). James Rachels (1999) combines ethics and morals in his statement that

> morality is, at the very least, the effort to guide one's conduct by reason—that is, to do what there are the best reasons for doing—while giving equal weight to the interests of each individual who will be affected by one's conduct. (p. 19)

Robert Exley (2004) cites Lawrence Hinman's definition of ethics as "the explicit, philosophical reflection on moral beliefs and practices . . . a conscious stepping back and reflecting on morality" (p. 10).

James Davis (2003) defines ethics as "the normative study of what people ought to do and why they should do it" (p. 116). He cites the work of Brincat and Wike, who make distinctions between morality and ethics, arguing that "morality is what people do and ethics is the study of what people ought to do; thus 'morality is like eating' and 'ethics is like nutrition'" (p. 116).

Ethics, then, examines the rational justification for moral judgments. Community college presidents are in a position to make moral judgments daily. Their decisions not only affect themselves and their personal and professional lives, but also have a considerable impact on the personal and professional lives of a host of internal and external constituents.

Ethical Perspectives _____

There are many ways to categorize the concept of ethics. A particularly useful system, devised by Craig Johnson (2005), looks at ethical approaches that can be practically applied by community college presidents. These ethical perspectives include utilitarianism, the categorical imperative, justice as fairness, communitarianism, altruism, and ethical pluralism.

Utilitarianism is a bedrock of democracy. Since it accepts that ethical choices should be based on their consequences, those choices should benefit the largest number of people possible. In other words, the majority rules. Utilitarianism is often described as "the greatest good for the greatest number." Thus, when issues of program priority surface, the utilitarian president would see that those programs benefiting the greatest number of students secure more resources than those benefiting a lesser number. Student clubs would be resourced based on the number of students who can benefit from the activity. Faculty who teach small numbers of students would not receive the same benefits as those who teach large numbers of students.

Unintended consequences, of course, would follow the use of utilitarianism in decision-making. Cutting-edge programs, new technologies, and specialized skills would be disregarded or minimized in a strictly utilitarian environment; so, too, would students with special needs and talents, leading to the undervaluing of diversity.

The *categorical imperative* stands in direct contrast to the utilitarian approach. It originated with the German philosopher Immanuel Kant, who argued that people should do the right thing regardless of the consequences. He saw a uniform set of rights and wrongs. According to this view, certain activities, such as lying, cheating, and killing, are always wrong, regardless of the context. Other activities, such as truth-telling and helpfulness, are always right. From this perspective, there are no little white lies.

Although on the surface this approach seems to encourage consistency and fairness, there are actually few principles that can be reasonably followed in every circumstance. Attempting to do so soon reveals all sorts of quandaries: Should one lie to save the life of a friend? Does an individual have the right to kill in time of war or for self-defense? Does a community college president advocate one set of rights and wrongs as appropriate at all times for all cultures? When dealing with competing businesses over a plant location, does a president have the responsibility, or even the right, to reveal confidential information if principle seems to require it? Should the president be concerned about a subordinate's self-image when it is time for annual personnel evaluations?

Justice as fairness is a matter of much dispute, particularly in democratic societies and in academic organizations. Is it ethical to reduce taxes on the rich in the hope that lower taxes will create more jobs? Is it ethical for a community college president to use affirmative action to advantage certain employees at the expense of others? Harvard political philosophy professor John Rawls "set out to identify principles that would foster cooperation in a society made up of free and equal citizens who, at the same time, must deal with inequalities" (Johnson, 2005, p. 135). Rawls identified two principles of justice he believed should be built into social institutions, including colleges (Johnson, p. 135):

> Principle 1: Each person has an equal right to the same basic liberties that are compatible with similar liberties for all.

> Principle 2: Social and economic inequalities are to satisfy two conditions: (A) They are to be attached to offices and positions open to all under conditions of fair equality of opportunity. (B) They are to be to the greatest benefit of the least advantaged members of society.

Thus, basic rights have priority, which means, for example, that all people must have freedom of speech and religion. Discrimination is illegitimate, and everyone should have access to the training and education needed to be successful.

Community colleges, with their open admissions policies, strive to meet this first basic principle. However, the difficulty comes in implementing the second principle, that those with the most need should have priority. In other words, while inequalities do exist, institutions and their leaders should prioritize the needs of traditionally marginalized groups, including minorities, immigrants, and the poor. These individuals would be the focus of the ethical president operating from the justice-as-fairness perspective. Thus, the president may decide more resources need to be devoted to developmental coursework, GED programs, or English as a Second Language programs.

Communitarianism suggests that everyone needs to shoulder responsibilities for the common, or community, good. This view emphasizes the creation of healthy communities with individuals assuming collective responsibilities, including staying informed about public issues and participating in community activities. "Communitarians," according to Johnson

(2005), "address the problems posed by competing interests by urging leaders and followers to put the needs of the whole above the needs of any one individual, group, or organization" (p. 139). For the community college president with a communitarian perspective, strategic planning and team leadership would be paramount. The focus would be on working with community organizations, social service agencies, and economic development entities for the good of the community. Of course, the communitarian president must not become so involved with external constituencies that the internal needs of the organization are neglected.

Altruism may be the most personally challenging of the ethical perspectives, since it suggests that "love of neighbor is the ultimate ethical standard. People are never a means to an end; they are the ends" (Johnson, 2005, p. 143). Thus, altruistic community college presidents always put others' needs ahead of their own. Leaders whose major interests are in promoting themselves quickly lose the respect of their followers. Those who would serve as altruistic community college presidents must understand that the needs of the college and the community come before their own needs—or those of their families. Altruism is reflected in the community college president's concern for the welfare of employees and students. Salary increases accrue to faculty and staff before the president. Student success, empathetic teaching, and a strong scholarship and financial aid program are all priorities of an altruistic president. While the altruistic community college president is so focused on the needs of others, there must be some balance. Always thinking of the needs of others may result in neglecting personal and professional needs for a healthy family life, for personal and professional development, and for exercise and reflective time.

Altruism, communitarianism, justice as fairness, the categorical imperative, and utilitarianism represent overlapping and sometimes conflicting ethical values. In most cases, the successful community college president must adapt and combine these perspectives in order to resolve ethical problems: He or she must pursue *ethical pluralism*. Such a president reflects on the various perspectives and from this knowledge develops a unique and individual personal ethical perspective or code of ethics. This approach represents an authentic and deliberative set of values that will guide the president through the inevitable ethical dilemmas endemic to the community college presidency. A personal code of ethics permits a president to consider ethical choices based on a substantive, well-thought-out plan rather than on what is merely convenient or expedient. Every leader, but particularly the president of a community college, should have a personal code of ethics that guides decision-making for the good of the college community as well as the larger community in which the college functions.

Ethical leadership is essential to gaining and keeping the trust not only of internal constituencies, but also of external constituencies, including funding agencies. Recognizing the impact of ethical leadership, the American Association of Community Colleges (AACC) proposed through its Presidents' Leadership Academy in November of 2005 a code of ethics for chief executive officers of community colleges. This code begins with a preamble that states, in part, the following:

> The Chief Executive Officer of the community college helps to determine ethical standards for his/her institution through personal conduct and institutional leadership . . . [and] is expected to maintain the highest ethical standards through individual actions and decisions within the institution and to expect adherence to the same standards by Boards of Trustees, administrators, faculty, staff and students. (AACC, 2005)

The document goes on to suggest that a set of core values will foster ethical standards that permeate the institution: "1. Trust and respect for all individuals; 2. Honesty in all actions; 3. Just and fair treatment of all people; 4. Integrity in all actions" (AACC, 2005). While other values specific to the institution and its history and needs may be added, the president must first promote these four core values in all institutional actions.

The Code of Ethics further details specific responsibilities to board members; responsibilities to administration, faculty, and staff; responsibilities to students; responsibilities to other educational institutions; and responsibilities to businesses, civic groups, and the community at large. It ends with a section on the rights of chief executive officers that include the right to clear expectations of performance from the board of trustees, the right to select the management team, the right to participate in setting goals and policies, and the right to a clear written contract that outlines conditions of employment, method of evaluation, and level of compensation (AACC, 2005).

Mythologies _____

Former community college president George Vaughan (1992) discusses four myths of ethics: 1) if it is legal, it is ethical; 2) if people have a right to do it, it is the right thing to do; 3) if people are not ethical by the time they are adults, it is too late for them to change; and 4) if people have a code of ethics, things will dramatically improve. The community college president must be cognizant of these myths in order to be an ethical leader.

First is the myth that if it is legal, it is ethical. Without a doubt, it is quite possible to behave within the letter of the law and still be unethical. Countless examples abound from business and industry, including the tobacco industry leaders swearing before Congress that their products are not addictive and the scandals of Enron and their ilk that recently filled news media. Financial malfeasance seems to be all too common in both business and higher education.

But there are also personnel practices that may be legal but not ethical. For example, many institutions do not have strict nepotism policies. Thus, while it may indeed be legal for the spouse of a governing board member to serve in a high-level administrative position within a college, the ethics of such a situation are questionable. What sort of atmosphere is created within such an administrative team? How does the president make difficult decisions in this circumstance for the good of the college? What questions lurk relative to presidential evaluation? The truly ethical president has at hand a well-thought-out personal code of ethics that goes beyond simply acting legally. Justice as fairness is one of the ethical values or perspectives that assures integrity and consideration of the needs of all groups in making institutional decisions and is an integral part of the AACC Code of Ethics.

The second myth is the belief that if people have a right to do it, it is the right thing to do. A president has tremendous positional authority. As such, a president may have the legal right to terminate an obnoxious employee who is basically competent but is critical of the president. But just because the president has the right, is this the right thing to do? A president may have the right to boost the salary of a small number of select staff; because the president has the right, is it the right thing to do? A president may have a First Amendment right to disclose the proceedings of a sensitive real estate venture handled in a closed-door session. But is this the right thing to do for the good of the organization? This may be where a president has the opportunity to demonstrate utilitarianism—being sure that the actions he or she takes do indeed benefit the majority of constituents, both within and beyond the college. Just and fair treatment of all people is one of the core values of the AACC Code of Ethics, a value that can foster ethical standards throughout the institution.

Third is the myth that if people are not ethical by the time they are adults, it is too late for them to change. Changing long-standing habits is certainly difficult. Nevertheless, being in the business of changing lives for the better, presidents need to see that ethical behavior is not just a matter of character, but also a matter of personal choice. On an individual and organizational level, a president must believe that everyone in the institution is capable of developing and adhering to mutually beneficial values. With practice and encouragement, people can learn to be more ethical in their decision-making. Few individuals can be absolutely ethical all the time, but a belief in education and learning should point toward more ethical behavior as individuals learn to accept and internalize the ethical values of the college. Of course, those values must be lived and demonstrated daily by the president. Altruism and communitarianism are significant ethical values in helping people to change for the better. As the AACC Code of Ethics makes clear, ethical example begins at the top, in that the CEO of the college helps to determine ethical standards for the institution through personal conduct and leadership.

The last myth is that if people have a code of ethics, things will dramatically improve. This is not necessarily so; there are no guarantees. However, the process of creating a code of ethics for an institution can be as important as the code itself. By promoting discussion and awareness, by putting ethical decision-making at the forefront of institutional values and planning, people will think more deeply about the implications of their decisions and will thereby be inclined to act more ethically.

A code of ethics such as that developed by the AACC for college presidents can be immensely helpful to all leaders, but just having the code of ethics is not sufficient. In fact, "ethical codes set forth by the states and professional associations tend to be limited in their responsiveness in that they are somewhat removed from the day-to-day personal and professional dilemmas educational leaders face" (Shapiro & Stefkovich, 2005, p. 21). At best, these codes serve as guideposts, and they model the ideals of the profession. To be effective and meaningful, however, the code of ethics must be exemplified by the president.

Ethical Issues_____

Countless ethical issues confront community college leaders in general and presidents in particular. Davis (2003) delineates a plethora of potential ethical issues that should be of concern to any president. There are ethical issues regarding student admissions, particularly in high-demand programs, in relation to equity and access, and there are issues around the availability of a variety of forms of financial aid. Colleges have not always held strictly to truth-in-marketing enrollment figures, placement of students, and other services and programs; colleges have not always handled well the appointment, promotion, and reward of faculty, or student/faculty relationships. Academic honesty, student grading and testing, classroom teaching, and the preparation of letters of recommendation for students are further potentially ethical issues, as are student-related concerns about academic honor codes, disciplinary processes, and tolerance of diversity in behavior, appearance, and values.

Institutional policies, created by boards and implemented by presidents, present another opportunity to examine the ethics of an institution. Are there well-established processes for reporting sexual harassment and criminal activities? Are there unambiguous due-process procedures in place? Are there clear expectations about the use of college property, including personal use of telephones, copy machines, and laptops? Are there clear expectations about Internet use, about college travel, and about reimbursement?

Outside the institution there are ethical issues related to community linkages and to business and industry alliances and partnerships. Are partnerships beneficial to all participants, or do they favor one or the other partner unduly? Is careful consideration given to partnerships with underrepresented groups as well as with those who represent mainstream business interests? Political issues are another potential land mine. There are political issues in relation to local, regional, and state policymakers; donations and appearances at fundraisers; and political activities on behalf of candidates. The ethical president needs to tread carefully here. Elective politics means the players, the decision makers, and the college funding sources can change by a decision of the voters. Most presidents prefer to avoid partisan politics because of the inherent danger that becoming too closely aligned with one party poses to the long-term well-being of the college.

Ethical issues are frequently raised in relation to governing boards. Do board members benefit financially through business interests relative to their position with the college? Are all possible conflicts of interest recognized and dealt with openly? Are there opportunities for undue influence regarding the hiring and firing of employees? Board members must act as a unit and not as individuals. Sunshine laws and open-meeting policies should be strictly observed. Ethical presidents support the professional development of their board members to help them understand the nature of their responsibilities and the importance of setting an example of unblemished ethics for the community in board deliberations and decision-making.

Another source of ethical dilemmas occurs with the growing need to raise funds to enhance the operations of the college, to support faculty, and to provide financial aid to students. How active should the president be in raising funds? What can the president promise to donors? What should and what should not be promised? How should funds be invested for the good of the college? Who should be selected as the college banking entity? Who is responsible for investment decisions? How does the president know that all such decisions are being made ethically, with the best interests of the college foremost?

Principles of Ethical Leadership

A conscientious and committed president will have spent the time necessary to understand the basic perspectives inherent in ethical leadership, including the mythologies of ethical presidential leadership and the ethical issues that challenge presidents in their professional lives. Northouse (2004) sets out the following five basic principles of ethical leadership that are directly applicable to the role of the community college president: respecting others, serving others, being just, being honest, and building community. These basic principles of ethical leadership closely parallel the ethical perspectives described earlier: the perspectives of utilitarianism, the categorical imperative, justice as fairness, communitarianism, and altruism. Further, Northouse's five principles mirror the AACC Code of Ethics in emphasizing the importance of respect and trust for all individuals, honesty, just and fair treatment, and integrity.

An ethical president respects others as ends, not as means to an end. The president is empathetic, tolerant, and gives credence to the views and interests of others both within and without the institution. The president is a good listener who is willing, when appropriate, to defer to others. Justice and fairness permeate discussions, decisions, and actions.

An ethical president serves others and puts others' needs above his or her own personal needs. The president exemplifies altruism, an ethic of caring for and about others. Employees are empowered to perform their work with a minimum of oversight. Mentoring is apparent as experienced employees assist new employees to become a part of the culture of the institution. Teams and team-building are valued. "Ethical leaders," argues Northouse (2004), "have a responsibility to attend to others, be of service to them, and make decisions pertaining to them that are beneficial and not harmful to their welfare" (p. 312).

An ethical president is just. Issues of fairness and justice are a top priority in dealing with faculty and staff. The distribution of resources within an institution reveals whether decisions are just; favoritism has no place. Inasmuch as resources are always finite and there is always competition for those resources, a just president must consider principles involved in distributive justice. These principles are applied in different situations and include allotting resources on the basis of equal shares, according to individual need, according to a person's rights, according to individual effort, according to societal contribution, and according to merit (Northouse, 2004).

An ethical president is honest. While this seems obvious, it is not always so easy. When a president is dishonest, the institution experiences distrust. The president may be seen as unreliable and not worthy of following. Honesty goes beyond simply telling the truth, even if it is painful. Honesty also implies an openness to discussing what matters to the institution and to employees. It means that decisions are based on evidence, that policies are clear, and that the budgeting process is transparent. An honest president is authentic, sensitive to the needs and feelings of others, and tempers honesty with consideration. An honest president will reward openly honest behavior within the organization and welcome information that may be negative or uncomfortable. An honest president does not shoot the messenger.

An ethical president builds community. The president recognizes that broader community needs must be attended to, both within the institution and the area served by the college. An ethical president recognizes that it is not beneficial in the long term to impose ideas and actions on others.

Rather, it is the role of the ethical president to be a transformational leader (Burns, 1978), moving both leaders and followers toward a common goal so that both are changed in a positive way. Burns suggests that successful leadership is grounded in the leader-follower relationship, which cannot be controlled solely by the leader and does not involve coercion. An ethical leader, furthermore, "takes into account the purposes of everyone involved in the group and is attentive to the interests of the community and the culture" (Northouse, 2004, p. 316). The president setting out to build community must work to assure that both individual and group goals support and sustain the public good.

A Call for Ethical Leaders

Consciously striving to live an ethical life is challenging by itself. But it is more challenging to carry, as the community college president does, the ethical responsibility for the well-being of both individuals and an institution. It is at once a tremendous privilege and opportunity, and a sometimes overwhelming burden. Those who occupy the community college presidency have a special responsibility because of their visibility in the community and their positional power to exercise that power ethically.

Ethical presidents are not perfect human beings. They make mistakes, but they acknowledge those mistakes. They set an example for the institution by showing respect for others, serving others, being just and honest, and building community. They have thoughtfully devised their own meaningful code of ethics, and this personal code underpins all the decisions they make. They are open in their dealings with colleagues and with leaders in the community. They demonstrate sensitivity to the needs of others, and they genuinely care about others.

Strong, strategic, and well-prepared community college presidents are needed to effectively serve the diverse and dynamic institutions that community colleges have become. Particularly in today's challenging political and fiscal environments, as colleges increasingly operate globally, they need presidents who are also dependable, trustworthy, honest, and open communicators. Tomorrow's successful president will be the leader who possesses not only strong experience and preparation, but also recognized ethical strengths. The community college president of the future will bridge the gap between theory and practice, exemplifying ethical leadership for the college and for the community.

References

American Association of Community Colleges. (2005). *Recommended code of ethics for chief executive officers of community colleges.* Retrieved January 26, 2007, from www.aacc.nche.edu/Template.cfm?Section=Position _Statements&Template=/InterestDisplay.cfm&InterestCategoryID=224

Burns, J. M. (1978). *Leadership.* New York, NY: Harper & Row.

Davis, J. R. (2003). *Learning to lead: A handbook for postsecondary administrators.* Westport, CT: Praeger.

Dewey, J. (1902). *The school and society.* Chicago, IL: University of Chicago Press.

Exley, R. (December/January 2004). Morality across the curriculum. *Community College Journal, 73*(4), 10–13.

Johnson, C. E. (2005). *Meeting the ethical challenges of leadership: Casting light or shadow* (2nd ed.). Thousand Oaks, CA: Sage.

Northouse, P. G. (2004). *Leadership: Theory and practice* (3rd ed.). Thousand Oaks, CA: Sage.

Rachels, J. (1999). *The elements of moral philosophy* (3rd ed.). New York, NY: McGraw-Hill.

Shapiro, J. P., & Stefkovich, J. A. (2005). *Ethical leadership and decision making in education: Applying theoretical perspectives to complex dilemmas* (2nd ed.). Mahwah, NJ: Lawrence Erlbaum.

Vaughan, G. B. (1992). *Dilemmas of leadership: Decision making and ethics in the community college.* San Francisco, CA: Jossey-Bass.

5

Why Presidents and Trustees Should Care About Ethics

Gary W. Davis

A trustee still remembers her shock and pain when an ordinarily friendly board colleague suddenly condemned her: "You're in a conflict of interest, and you know that perfectly well!" he virtually shouted. Only later did she learn that her fellow trustees resented her serving as the real estate agent in the college president's purchase of a new home.

"I didn't ask to show him houses," the trustee told herself. "Everybody knows that I sell real estate. I have a good feel for prices and locations here in town. The new president came to me and asked me if I would show him some houses. How can this be? I was just trying to help, to do a good deed, actually. We all wanted this president to get off to a good start, and I knew that if he found the right house, his family would fall in love with our town. How could it be wrong to help him and his family?"

The answer to this question, of course, is that the road to hell has always been paved with good intentions. In a flash, the well-intentioned trustee learned that even though she had no malicious intentions, her actions were judged improper by those she valued most: her fellow trustees.

This trustee had overestimated her ethical I.Q. Because she was guided by common sense, she thought she was on safe ground when she helped the college president find a new home. After all, she knew real estate, and the president needed good advice. Just because they are experienced and generally savvy people, trustees can easily become the victims of ethical stumbling blocks. A *New Yorker* cartoon shows Satan coaching his demons:

"First," the devil says, "we lure them into self-righteousness!" One of the quickest ways to stumble ethically is to have a feeling of moral invincibility. Those who are sure that their decisions and actions will always be above reproach set themselves up for the fall.

As a result, more than one trustee has ended his or her own political career by acting unethically. Sometimes the improper behavior is that of one or two trustees. Just as often, the ethical breakdown involves an action of the entire board. It should not surprise anyone that boards and their members fall prey to ethical dilemmas. Well advised by attorneys and financial experts when dealing with legal and financial matters, board members are usually on their own when it comes to personal ethical decision-making. Ordinarily, no one advises the board on matters pertaining to ethics and ethical behavior.

Ethical pitfalls also await unsuspecting college presidents. Investigations of improprieties by college presidents involving, for example, personal and travel expenses, hiring practices, and sexual harassment are routinely reported in *The Chronicle of Higher Education* and *Community College Week*. Often, what went wrong in such situations is that the president depended on his or her own judgment exclusively to determine the propriety of the action, and this judgment failed him or her.

Unethical behavior is one of the quickest and surest ways for college presidents to lose their jobs. While some presidents are fired because they break the law, and others are dismissed because they fail to rally the faculty or the alumni, most are fired because they have lost the trust of their boards. Trust develops when people believe that those around them can be counted on to do the right thing. When presidents can no longer be trusted in this way, their days in office are numbered. Like their boards, presidents often function without the benefit of ethical advisors. Although they have financial officers and college attorneys to consult when the question before them involves budgets or the law, presidents facing ethical dilemmas usually have no one to rely on but themselves. For that very reason, presidents, as much as trustees, can benefit from a method for ethical decision-making.

What Is Ethical Behavior?

Ethical behavior involves more than legal behavior. The terms *ethics* and *morals* come from Greek and Latin roots that mean "commonly accepted behavior." In philosophy, ethics involves the study of the good. Some good behaviors are written into law, so that what began as an ethical concern turns out to be a legal one. For example, the ethical notion that it is wrong to deprive another of his or her property without due process has been converted into a law that prohibits theft. In cases such as these, the law echoes and encapsulates our notions of good and bad.

In many other cases, however, the law is silent. Consider, for example, a person driving down a street who notices someone trying to enter the flow of traffic from an adjoining alley. The first driver is not compelled by the law to stop his or her car in order to allow the second driver to enter the stream of traffic. Yet that is exactly what many drivers would do. When drivers voluntarily assist others on the road, they are responding to a moral or ethical norm called courtesy. Some human behavior is driven by a desire to act legally. Much more human behavior, however, results from people's desire to "do the right thing." In that sense, ethics comes into play more often than the law.

How Do Trustees and Presidents Fall Prey to Ethical Stumbling Blocks?_____

College presidents and trustees operate in a world full of potential ethical catastrophes. Unless one has been its victim before, an ethical dilemma may not be recognized when it appears. Of course, the time to become aware of ethical issues is before they end one's career or one's term of public service. Not every ethical dilemma is listed here, but the examples offered should enable readers to use their imagination and identify challenges that may confront them in the future.

1. Presidents and boards can fall prey to the truth-or-reputation dilemma.

Because they want to put the college's best foot forward, trustees and presidents sometimes are hesitant to tell the public the whole truth about the college. In part because community colleges have often been disparaged as second-rate institutions, community college leaders are especially sensitive about institutional reputation. For that reason alone, most community college boards feel uncomfortable talking about retention and graduation rates. Some boards are not comfortable discussing the fact that many, if not most, of their students are studying at precollegiate levels. Community college leaders may not be comfortable discussing heavy institutional reliance on part-time faculty. When a college's percentage of minority students and faculty fails to reflect the minority population of the local community, the college's leadership may hesitate to talk publicly about the need for more minority students, faculty, and staff. Some boards feel uncomfortable talking about the success rate of their college athletes. Every board has some issue that will be uncomfortable to discuss in public.

One of the reasons presidents and trustees fall prey to unethical behavior is that they can conduct much of their work in secret. Despite the fact that many states have sunshine laws that require the work of the public to be done in public, many boards find ways to conduct business out of the public's view.

There are, of course, some advantages to closed sessions. Parliamentary procedure is not required so people can have a no-holds-barred discussion about the subject at hand. Yet if the board is not open in dealing with challenges facing the college, the public eventually loses trust in the board, the president, and the college. Just as boards insist on the rule of "no surprises" in dealing with the college president, the people of the local district do not like to be surprised by stories in the media about problems at the college. Studies in the wake of scandals surrounding entities like Tylenol, the Red Cross, and the United Way show that the public will not lose faith with institutions that admit their problems and find solutions. The Watergate and Monica Lewinsky stories, on the other hand, demonstrate that the public soon loses faith in people and organizations that make a habit of hiding the truth. Whenever trustees or presidents are faced with bad news about their college, they should ask themselves whether there is a way to share the news with the public in a manner that builds trust.

Sometimes candor is turned into an idol. When a person is appointed or elected to a board on a reform ticket, fishing expeditions sometimes result as the new trustee looks for documentation to embarrass the college for purely political reasons. Similarly, in cleaning up messes created by their predecessors, new presidents sometimes create new problems for the college by unnecessarily exposing bad but trivial decisions from the past. In such cases, the reformer may be tempted to make an example of someone within the college or someone on the previous college board. Reformers have been known to make public personnel records and other materials that expose the college to legal risk. When the reformer puts retribution and personal political aspiration above every other interest, he or she can easily do permanent damage to a college's reputation. Before long, the public can be made to believe the entire college has been tainted by the acts of a few.

When boards or presidents are faced with cleaning up messes that their predecessors have created, the ethical question is, "Who has a right to know what?" Without a reliable method for sorting this issue out, it is not an easy question to answer.

2. Inertia can become the enemy of responsible behavior.

All boards and presidents experience pressure to maintain the status quo. Yet past practice may not have been responsible practice. Many a president has erred merely by continuing a practice that his or her predecessors used. Just because a certain behavior was accepted in the past does not mean it will be found acceptable in the future. Boards and presidents need to know that moral conventions change, and those who rely on past practice as a guide to behavior run the risk of offending a new morality.

For example, it was once not uncommon for executives to court and date their secretaries. In fact, to previous generations, the practice seemed charming and appropriate. In the past, some board members had romantic relationships with members of the college staff. Other trustees eventually married college employees. Today, such relationships are questioned because they may involve the abuse of a power relationship: The executive can have his or her secretary fired; does that leave the secretary free to resist advances? A board member may share the board's collective bargaining strategy with his or her college-employee spouse. From the other side, if the faculty union discovers the board's strategy, what are the chances the leak will be attributed to the trustee and his or her employee spouse?

Some presidents have fallen prey to ethical scandals that were orchestrated by their predecessors. Consider the case of the college president whose basketball coaches were cheating. Other presidents have become the victims of a shady college foundation they inherited when they took the job. Some presidents have discovered fraudulent activity in the financial aid department; if the fraud is small and likely not to be discovered, and if it works to the advantage of the students and the college, would most new presidents take on the task of cleaning up the mess, or would they just look the other way? When is a cleanup called for, and how long can reform be delayed while other, more urgent fires are being fought? Presidents need to know.

Just like presidents, trustees may be misled when they let themselves be guided by the board's past practice. In the early days of community colleges, presidents and board chairs often formed close personal friendships. They spent countless hours with each other, not only in the boardroom, but also on the golf course and at the local country club. Today's board may look askance at such a cozy relationship between one trustee and the college's chief executive officer. If the board chair and the president are close personal friends, can the board chair be objective when it comes time to evaluate the performance of the president? If the president's friend is another member of the board, does one board member get more information than the others do?

Contemporary levels of ethical sensitivity must guide today's presidents and trustees. They simply cannot afford to follow all the practices of previous boards and chief executives.

3. Presidents and boards can become the victims of tension between academic and real-world values.

Yet another danger to the reputation of college presidents stems from their close connection to academic culture. With its emphasis on human dignity and diversity, American academic culture affirms the right of every person to learn. Believing in the capacity of every student, presidents may be unwilling to set limits on the college's role or mission. Trustees and politicians, on the other hand, reflect the hard-nosed realism of the marketplace: Perhaps in any student cohort, some will not succeed no matter how much special help they receive; perhaps some student behavior and personal dress do fall below the threshold of social acceptability. In other words, trustees often recognize a human capacity for failure and for antisocial behavior. On the other hand, presidents often honor diversity, tolerate behavior that is shocking to some, and strive to avoid declaring any student a failure no matter what.

For some trustees, the fact that students occasionally fail may be reason enough to overlook the causes of failure. When they fail, at-risk students may be lacking the social, cultural, and academic support that the college could provide. Trustees who believe some students are destined to fail may be ignoring the effectiveness of special programs that can rescue the at-risk student. Real-world trustees may also question the value of total academic freedom, free inquiry, and free speech. Trustees who come from the workaday world will worry about grade inflation more than most faculty do. What should presidents do when they are challenged by their boards to "fix the problem of grade inflation"? The closer the trustees' value systems are to those of mainstream society, the harder it will be for those trustees to resonate with the values of the academy. When the values of the real world collide with the values of the academy, relationships are tested, and both the board and the college are at risk.

4. Boards and presidents face tensions between the demands of the marketplace and academic standards.

There will be times when presidents and boards are asked to make exceptions to college standards for the sake of the college's position in the marketplace. Most boards would put faculty staffing above almost any other need of the college. However, if colleges are judged by the quality of the weight rooms that they offer students, does a board have any choice but to ensure the college is as well equipped as its competitors? If the college's investment is not producing a winning football team, is there any choice but to invest more until the win-loss record improves? When parents demand special accommodations for their children, does a president have any recourse except to grant the parents their wish? But, of course, if done often enough, the action will put the college's enrollment in jeopardy.

What position will the board and the president take when faced with marketplace pressures? If "everybody else is doing it," will the college follow suit? If other colleges in the athletic conference are fraudulently paying student athletes, can the president and the board afford to insist that their college play by the rules? How much resistance to current practice is the board willing to show? If studies show that college students like to obtain and use credit cards, would the board support a plan to offer the students a credit card that pays 1% of each purchase to the college foundation? On the surface, the offer looks like a good deal for the students and the college alike—but *is* it good for the students? Does the fact that the college is capitalizing on a trend make the decision a good one?

5. There is a lack of ethical consensus in our pluralistic society.

One of the things that make ethical decision-making difficult for boards and presidents is the lack of ethical consensus in our society. Is a benefit for the individual more important than a benefit for the group? Is justice more important than mercy? Should resources be used today or saved for a time in the future when they might be needed more? Which is more important, telling the truth or showing concern for everyone involved? Cultural groups and individuals differ in their answers to these questions. Members of a board of trustees will differ as well.

How important is the college's partnership with the military? Branches of the military may want to come to campus to recruit students, but many faculty members may object to their presence on campus. Some faculty and students may wish to display symbols of their religious commitments on campus. Others may object to such displays. Some students and faculty may object to the presence of controversial speakers on campus, while other faculty and students see this as an issue of freedom of speech and the free exchange of ideas.

Trustees sometimes find themselves at each other's throats because they have not hammered out a set of core values to guide the board and the college. When one trustee believes that all students can learn and another believes that learning can only be accomplished by those who have a personal and cultural predisposition for it, angry encounters result. Unless the board has adopted a set of core values, ethical disagreements can seriously disrupt the board's processes.

6. Boards sometimes have to decide between benefiting local vendors and making a profit for the college.

Colleges sell more than classroom education. Many colleges sell health club memberships, eyeglasses, dental care, milk products, golf privileges, and cultural events, in addition to sweatshirts and books. Most community colleges sell a variety of products that students could also purchase from local vendors. Arguments can always be made that the college's sale of goods and services provides its students with a convenient venue for their purchase. Taxpaying businesses within the district, however, may have a different view. Why should they pay taxes for the support of the college and then have the college become a direct competitor? As long as books and supplies are readily available at a for-profit store across the street from the college, why should the college insist on operating its own bookstore? In fact, colleges sell goods and services in auxiliary enterprises that are nonacademic profit centers. Proceeds earned in such enterprises are used to underwrite the expense of the parts of colleges that traditionally lose money.

Another area in which colleges sometimes prioritize financial gain is its investment program. College officials may wish to create large fund balances both for the interest they accrue and for the financial flexibility large investments offer: Rather than having to rely on the changeable political entities that appropriate money to the college, presidents and trustees can simply dip into their own reserves when they have a pressing need.

But college officials are not alone in being faulted for stashing away reserves far in excess of what might be needed to meet an emergency. In the summer of 2005, Blue Cross of Tennessee was faulted for having a $1 billion reserve while its members' medical costs were skyrocketing. Should students pay higher rates of tuition when the board is putting money aside for a rainy day? Presidents and trustees can easily be accused of making self-serving decisions in their handling of money. It is not hard for a board and a president to overlook the needs of tuition-paying students when they decide to compile a large reserve fund. On the other hand, an adequate reserve fund can stabilize the college's growth. How will trustees learn to resolve the dilemma that pits the students' immediate needs against the college's long-range growth?

7. Boards and presidents are sometimes tempted to bend the law.

Although ethics transcends the law, one value that most communities hold is that of obedience to the statutes of the nation and state. Over the past three decades, Congress and the state legislatures have passed thousands of laws regulating the operation of public colleges. Some laws require that teachers speak good English. Other statutes dictate refund policies that colleges must use when settling the accounts of students who have dropped out of school. For Congress and the legislatures, no part of college life can seem too trivial to be excluded from regulation.

This increasing regulatory burden has become costly for colleges, and it has made regulatory management more difficult. Now, when a president decides how to handle a difficult situation, he or she must consider not only what is good for the students and the college, but also what is required by statute. And, as states relentlessly regulate public colleges and universities, institutions look for clever ways to evade regulation. For example, if a state collects the college's tuition but not its fees, a board may decide to freeze its tuition rate and substantially increase student fees instead. Is this an evasion of the state legislature's intent? Probably. Is it legal? Probably. So what should the board do?

Whenever college presidents and boards engage in creative applications of state laws to evade the spirit of those laws, they invite condemnation by the legislature and the press. On the other hand, to ignore the latitude that some of the regulations afford the college is to sacrifice promising management options. Presidents and boards will always face this question: How far should the president and the board go in finding ways around or through the morass of current regulation? The question is not only what is legal, but what is ethical.

8. Boards and presidents sometimes violate the duties of loyalty, care, and obedience.

In their orientation briefings, new trustees are often encouraged to consider the board's duties of loyalty, care, and obedience. The duty of obedience requires the board to act in accordance with the laws of the land and the board's own policies. Unless the board suffers from having an incompetent legal advisor or a disorganized and contradictory set of policies, it can fulfill its duty of obedience without great difficulty. The duty of care can be met when board members make an effort to study board materials and to attend board meetings regularly.

Of the three duties, the duty of loyalty is the one most likely to confound a board. This duty demands that board members not engage in self-dealing: The board is to act on behalf of the college, not on behalf of the trustees. Whenever a board approves its own travel expenditures, the duty of loyalty hangs in the balance. What prevents the board from squandering precious college resources on its own fine dining and first-class treatment by airlines and hotels?

No group except the board of trustees can approve trustee expenditures; therefore, some degree of self-dealing is unavoidable. Trustee development requires trustee travel. Were a board to refuse to approve its own expenses for its development, it would violate its duty of care. The board would suffer, and the college would ultimately pay the price for an under-prepared, undereducated board of trustees.

Fortunately, there are ways a board can ensure that its own expenses are reasonable and related to the college's welfare. The board can adopt a policy that trustee expenditures that are not preapproved will not be paid. When such a policy is in effect, trustees must seek the approval of the board chair (or a board development committee) before incurring expenses related to their travel. Another way boards can ensure that board expenses are reasonable is to open them to public scrutiny. By discussing board travel expenses in public sessions, the board members show that they are not ashamed of incurring these expenses and that they have nothing to hide.

Unfortunately, some boards and presidents have found ways to conceal improper expenditures. Just as legislators sometimes use automatic raise statutes to give themselves raises quietly, college trustees can enrich themselves out of the public view. For example, a president may be tempted to show the trustees a little of the good life when he or she and the board travel together. Often board travel arrangements are made in the president's office, and the president can easily book five-star hotels and restaurants when less extravagant accommodations would do just as well. When the board is treated this way, the board members can become informally indebted to the president. As a result, they may be less likely to oversee the president regularly and rigorously. The president and the board can become friendly to the point that the trustees' loyalty may be called into question. If a president has arranged for luxurious accommodations for the board, will the board question the president's "professional" winter trip to a tropical location? Meeting planners know that conferences for presidents and trustees sell out when they are scheduled for choice locations during the high season. What is the board's responsibility for seeing that presidential and board development activities are purchased at a reasonable rate?

Sometimes trustees and presidents fall prey to the charge of self-dealing even as they try to do a favor for the college. When trustees permit college departments to perform services on the trustees' automobiles or homes in order for students to gain experience, the trustees expose themselves to the charge that they are profiting from their role as members of the board. When presidents ask the college staff to work on their private residences to prepare the home for a college-related reception, they expose themselves to the charge that they are profiting unethically at the expense of the college. When presidents ask those who report to them to sign for presidential expenses, they effectively guarantee that the expenditure will be approved. They have, in effect, approved their own expenditure of college funds.

Should a president's spouse be employed at the college? Can other college employees honestly believe that the president's spouse does not receive special treatment because he or she is married to the college president? Should a person serve as a trustee if a member of his or her immediate family works at the college? This is a difficult call. Illinois case law makes clear that it is unfair to prohibit employment to a person simply because the person's spouse is on the board of the college. Thus, in Illinois, it is quite legal for a trustee's spouse to work at the college. But is it ethical? Might those in the community not believe that the spouse got the job (or is able to retain the job) because he or she is married to a board member? The issue grows even more complex for colleges in small towns with limited talent pools. If a trustee's daughter is the most qualified to teach at the college, should she not be hired when there is a vacancy that calls for her talents?

One might think any reasonable trustee or president would be able to foresee and avoid situations that might constitute a conflict of interest, but this is not the case. Often the last person to see a conflict of interest is the person who is most directly involved in it. For that reason, trustees and presidents need to monitor and coach each other. When a trustee sees a situation that might be construed as a conflict of interest, he or she should not assume that the person involved in the potential conflict knows exactly what he or she is doing. Rather, the trustee should let the person who may be in a conflict know about what might become a problem once others become aware of the situation.

9. Tension exists between candor and respect.

Because they do not want to offend each other, trustees and the president are often hesitant to share ethical concerns. Many are afraid that if an ethical concern is raised, the person who raises it will be resented. Worse yet, the person who voices an ethical concern may well get a taste of his or her own medicine by being judged more harshly by fellow board members in the future. If stung by the perception that a fellow trustee doubts his or her integrity, a board member may well look for a chance to "even the score" when the accuser suffers a possible ethical lapse.

Most boards and presidents do not take the time to work out protocols for use when someone has a concern about possibly unethical behavior. Leaks from closed sessions plague every board, yet few boards have a policy and procedure for addressing leaks when they occur. It is one thing to have a policy prohibiting unethical behavior, but quite another to have a procedure for dealing with that behavior if it appears. Most boards have policies; few have protocols that are written, understood, and readily available when a potential problem arises.

10. Ethics presents a challenge at the systems level.

In the wake of Hurricane Katrina, President Michael A. MacDowell of College Misericordia in Pennsylvania told *The Chronicle of Higher Education* in 2005 that colleges and universities often lack a plan when it comes time to help their communities:

> While many campuses have plans that consider such resources and service-learning opportunities, few of those plans are sufficiently integrated with their metropolitan, regional, and state emergency-management agencies' crisis plans. Whether you are part of a large system or just one campus, successful emergency management requires better coordination and training than currently exists at most institutions. (p. B16)

President MacDowell's observation shows that sometimes people are prevented from doing the right thing because of the systems that guide, shape, and enable the behavior of individuals. When the systems are obsolete, broken, or missing, responsible actions are either impossible or much less likely to occur.

Many community colleges do not have working relationships with the high schools that prepare their students. Many community colleges do not get regular and reliable feedback on the performance of their transfer students because the college lacks an effective working relationship with the universities to which students transfer. When systems break down, people are harmed, and sooner or later someone goes looking for a culprit. In the case of the college that was not prepared to help its community after a natural disaster, the problem is traced back to the lack of a system to link town and gown. In the case of high school or community college students who arrive at their next school unprepared to do the work expected of them, the problem is traced back to the lack of a seamless educational web.

In cases where systems break down, the finger of blame is usually pointed at the educational leaders who failed to anticipate the need for structures that would permit people to collaborate on the solution of shared problems. In *Moral Man and Immoral Society* (2005), the American theologian Reinhold Niebuhr observed that good people are capable of doing great evil. Even when a community is made up of noble individuals, if the system within which they live is corrupt, disaster will result. To build just communities and nations, people must learn the craft of system-building and policymaking.

Yet many people who join a community college board have no experience in either task. Although trustees deserve assistance in acquiring the skills necessary for effective and ethical policymaking, most boards lack a rigorous plan for trustee development. When trustees reduce ethics to the behavior of individuals, and they exclude systematic deficiencies from their analyses, ethical decision-making will never be sufficient to the tasks that face a college board. In order to fully perform their proper role for a president or a board, a system of ethics must be applicable to the world of policy as well as the world of individual behavior.

Conclusion

College trustees and presidents need and deserve a method for making decisions ethically. Practically every decision made by a college president or trustee involves some sort of ethical choice. Should the money be spent now or saved for later? Should we support our community or take care of our own? Shall we tell the truth or protect those involved? Shall we demand justice or simply put the matter behind us? In Chapter 13 of this text, "A Guide to Ethical Decision-Making by Presidents and Boards," I move from the need of trustees and presidents for a system for ethical decision-making to eight simple questions they can ask in order to make ethical decisions, with each question allowing them to analyze the ethical content of their decisions.

References

MacDowell, M. A. (2005, September 9). Prepared to help when disaster strikes. *The Chronicle of Higher Education,* p. B16.

Niebuhr, R. (2005). *Moral man and immoral society* (New ed.). New York, NY: Continuum International.

6

Professional Ethical Identity Development and Community College Leadership

Sharon K. Anderson, Clifford P. Harbour, Timothy Gray Davies

The development of community college leaders has been addressed from a variety of perspectives. Brown, Martinez, and Daniel (2002) and Townsend and Bassoppo-Moyo (1997) have discussed competencies appropriate for community college leaders. Anderson, Murray, and Olivarez (2002) and McArthur (2002) have focused on the various roles of community college leaders. Amey, VanDerLinden, and Brown (2002) and Miller and Pope (2003) have reported on empirical studies of leadership career paths. Finally, Baker (2002), Davies and Quick (2001), and Lovell, Crittenden, Stumpf, and Davis (2003) have examined a variety of program models currently used in graduate leadership development programs. These contributions all explicitly or implicitly acknowledge the need for ethical community college leadership. However, research and commentary focusing on the ethical dimension of community college leadership is limited. Notable exceptions include works by Anderson and Davies (2000), Baker (1992), and Vaughan (1992).

The absence of a rich literature on ethical leadership at community colleges is significant. Practitioners know successful leadership requires the resolution of ethical dilemmas under trying circumstances. Presidents, trustees, and other campus leaders make critical decisions with ethical significance daily (Anderson & Davies, 2000; Baker, 1992; Vaughan, 1992). New political, economic, and technological conditions create novel ethical

61

dilemmas for community college leaders. In some cases, leaders may not be prepared to resolve them, and fundamental community college principles such as open access, the comprehensive mission, student success, and service to the community may be at risk.

For instance, the widespread adoption of institutional accountability programs may cause campus leaders to consider tempering their commitment to these principles so that they can report "better results" to state officials (Harbour & Nagy, 2005). Funding challenges may tempt campus administrators to reduce the ranks of full-time faculty even when academic program reviews indicate a need for such staffing. Finally, the advent of distance learning technologies may bring its own ethical challenges. College officials may be pushed to adopt low-cost/high-revenue online programs to serve students in faraway places even though an assessment of community workforce conditions may clearly indicate the need for on-campus, high-cost/low-revenue programs.

In this chapter, we focus on a dimension of ethics and community college leadership that has not been addressed: the need for formal professional ethical identity development initiatives to support community college leaders. We address this need by proposing a framework for understanding community college leaders' professional ethical identity development. We explain how this framework may be incorporated into a variety of community college leadership development programs, including graduate programs, statewide leadership academies, and institutional professional development initiatives. This framework builds on Berry's (1980; 2003; Berry & Sam, 1997) model of acculturation as well as recent scholarship on professional ethical identity by Handelsman, Gottlieb, and Knapp (2005).

To these ends, we have organized our discussion in the following manner. First, we outline Berry's model of acculturation and describe its relevancy to community college leadership. Second, we explain how Handelsman et al. (2005) adapted Berry's model of acculturation to explain how professionals (e.g., psychologists) may use one of four strategies to establish a professional ethical identity. This identity is developed by resolving tension between the leader's personal values and the fundamental community college principles. Third, we focus on one particular strategy, the integration strategy, and offer a vignette demonstrating the construction of a professional ethical identity. Finally, we explain how community college leadership development programs may help future leaders understand and apply this integrative strategy, thus securing their own professional ethical identity.

The Berry Model of Acculturation _____

Berry and Sam (1997) have explained that a psychological acculturation process occurs when an individual encounters people from a different culture. When individuals have this experience, they effectively make two decisions: the first concerns maintaining his or her culture of origin, including its values, beliefs, and ways of knowing; the second concerns connecting with the new culture and its values, beliefs, and ways of knowing. These two decisions occur simultaneously and result in the adoption of one of four acculturation strategies: assimilation, separation, integration, or marginalization.

Berry and Sam (1997) implicitly recognized what Anderson, Wagoner, and Moore (2006) explicitly stated about specific organizations and professions: Each organization or profession has its own professional culture, comprised of its history, its traditions and values, the philosophical views of its leaders, its accepted membership criteria, its shared language, its written and unwritten ethical codes or standards of practice, and the training sanctioned or required by the organization or profession.

Conceptualization of Professional Ethical Identity _____

Handelsman et al. (2005) developed the professional ethical identity concept based on the psychological acculturation work of Berry (1980, 2003) and Berry and Sam (1997). Handelsman et al. used their conceptualization of psychological acculturation as a guide to describing how new professionals become a part of and adapt to a new organization or profession and adjust to its ethical culture. They claimed this adjustment was best understood as an acculturation strategy.

Following Berry and Sam (1997), and with only modest theoretical revision, Handelsman et al. (2005) identified four possible responses to the acculturation experience: assimilation, separation, marginalization, and integration. Their revision had two components. First, to accommodate their concern with professional ethical identity development, they focused on an individual's personal value system, which replaced Berry and Sam's attention to an individual's culture of origin. Thus, for Handelsman et al., the tension is not between a person's culture of origin and the new organizational culture, but between the individual's personal values (which probably come from his or her culture of origin) and the new organization's endorsed values.

The professional ethical identity process concerns accepting or rejecting the professional values of the new organization and its culture in light of the individual's personal values. Therefore, in the second component of their revision, Handelsman et al. (2005) concluded that appropriate professional ethical identity development is contingent on the strategy used by an individual to resolve the tension between organizational and personal values. Keeping in mind this two-part revision to the Berry and Sam (1997) model, we summarize briefly the four responses describing how new professionals adapt to a new organization and adjust to its ethical culture.

Assimilation

When individuals adopt an assimilation strategy, they exhibit less interest in maintaining their personal values than in connecting with and adopting the new professional values and standards of the organization. People adopting this ethical identity development strategy distance themselves from a personal sense of right and wrong (their personal moral code) and embrace the new organization's professional ethics without examination and critical reflection. As Handelsman et al. (2005) suggest, these individuals may have little or no personal sense of ethics, or they may believe that becoming part of the profession or organization means giving up their personal values because their ethics are not relevant or helpful to the new professional identity. Simply stated, they begin their journey in the new professional culture with a limited personal ethical foundation.

Separation

Individuals exhibit the separation strategy when they adhere to their personal values and discount new professional values and standards. These individuals would typically have a well-developed personal code of ethics or strong beliefs about right and wrong behavior, and/or a limited understanding or acceptance of the new organization's professional values. These individuals may be marginal members in the new culture and uninitiated into its values and ethics. Alternatively, they may believe their way is the right way because it is based on an ethical perspective acquired in a previous professional culture.

Marginalization

Handelsman et al. (2005) suggest that marginalization could be the most problematic acculturation strategy for individuals developing a professional ethical identity. Here individuals have limited interest in *either* maintaining their personal values *or* connecting to or integrating with the new organization's professional values and standards. Considered in the context of ethical identity development, these persons are adrift. They have weak ties to ethical values acquired in their earlier personal and social settings and groups, and they have little interest in their new organization's professional ethics. When difficult ethical situations arise, these persons make decisions based on short-term concerns. They might make the right choice in specific cases, but over time, they will make ethical decisions based on convenience alone.

Integration

The integration strategy offers individuals the greatest potential for developing a constructive professional ethical identity (Handelsman et al., 2005). According to Berry and Sam (1997), "Evidence strongly supports a positive correlation between the use of this strategy and good psychological adaptation during acculturation" (p. 298). People who adopt this approach choose to retain important parts of their personal values while they internalize moral beliefs and practices their new organization endorses. These individuals integrate their new organization's professional ethical values while acknowledging their own core personal values. Handelsman et al. suggest that although these people may encounter conflicts between their personal sense of right and wrong and the standards and values endorsed by the new profession, they will be aware of the tensions and "work to resolve them in ways that foster greater integration" (p. 61).

We would add that one way these people will make ethical decisions is by questioning weakly supported professional values as well as rethinking loosely grounded personal values. They acknowledge their potential for flawed ethical thinking, and they acknowledge the potential for superficial ethical reasoning in their new organization. In short, they seek to make better ethical decisions in their work.

Integration: The Path to Professional Ethical Identity Development _____

In developing community college leaders, we propose that practitioners and researchers accept professional ethical identity development as a vital process for preparing these leaders for the challenges that lie ahead. In particular, we believe a focus on professional ethical identity development will assist community college leaders in retaining the positive values of democracy's college, while allowing for the innovation that must occur if these institutions are to succeed and thrive in future decades. An integration strategy practiced by community college leaders would help them endorse open access, the comprehensive mission, student success, and service to the community while accepting positive change.

We acknowledge that promotion of integration strategies for community college leaders will not be easy. Institutions will need to help leaders reconcile their personal values with the fundamental principles of community college education. This reconciliation will require that campus leaders respect the values and experiences new employees bring to campus even when they appear out of step with the college's traditions. Moreover, college leaders will need to accept responsibility for leadership succession and, more specifically, sharing established community college values with new employees.

We recognize that harmonizing personal and institutional values requires that the two not be too far apart. But in unusual circumstances, new leaders may bring personal values that cannot and should not be integrated into organizational culture. For example, it would be very difficult to reconcile a leader's belief in benevolent patriarchy with core community college values such as open access—so difficult, in fact, that attempting to do so may be regarded as futile.

Similarly, we contend that organizational values may also be corrupt or unjust, and that in such cases new leaders should reject integration strategies attempting to harmonize these values with their personal beliefs. Perhaps an institution implicitly endorses gender discrimination in hiring and promoting faculty. This endorsement must be confronted, condemned, and rejected. In short, integration requires more than attempting to reconcile any set of personal beliefs and community college values; it requires that both personal beliefs and college values be recognizable as reasonable ideals. Given these conditions, we offer the following vignette as an illustration of how a campus leader might develop an integration strategy.

Henrietta Higgins and Heartland Community College

The New Program Director

A year and a half ago, Henrietta Higgins was hired as a new program director at Heartland Community College (HCC). In this position, Henrietta is responsible for scheduling, staffing, and assessing HCC's English and social science courses and their instructional quality. Henrietta came to HCC after working at Flagship University for 15 years. Flagship is the state's premier research university and is widely regarded as having an exceptional university faculty and the region's most selective undergraduate and graduate programs. Henrietta received her Ph.D. at Flagship, and when a nontenure position opened up in her unit, she was appointed.

While at Flagship, Henrietta held a number of positions in the English department but never left her nontenure status. Instead, her initial appointment evolved into an administrative position with limited teaching responsibility and no responsibility for research and publication. Eventually, Henrietta was given responsibility for scheduling and staffing lower-division English courses and was widely regarded in the unit as a talented and energetic line administrator. However, when a series of unusually severe budget cuts required Flagship to start eliminating faculty positions, Henrietta was forced to seek employment elsewhere.

Henrietta had a smooth transition to HCC and quickly grew to enjoy her work and her new colleagues. Nevertheless, on occasion, she was somewhat uneasy with HCC's explicit commitment to open access and the comprehensive mission. In her eyes, these values required that HCC make concessions regarding academic integrity. For example, Henrietta had concerns about the college's open access policy because it resulted in the enrollment of students who would founder academically and require additional faculty time. She had reservations about HCC's comprehensive mission because it limited increases to program budgets like English and social science in order to support new programs serving emerging needs in the business and health care communities.

Henrietta was honest and forthright about her reservations in HCC's Academic Council meetings. When she would speak her mind on these issues, two groups of her fellow program directors would grin and exchange knowing glances among themselves, but for opposite reasons. A few program directors would grin because they believed Henrietta was beginning to understand HCC's greatest limitation: She now saw, as they did, that HCC was trying to serve students and accomplish ends beyond the reach of any public higher education institution. However, the larger group of program directors grinned because they believed Henrietta was beginning to truly understand that the community college's purpose was to serve students and meet community needs, even under extremely challenging conditions. These program directors were committed to open access and the comprehensive mission for a variety of reasons. But all of them agreed that the college's students were entitled to educational opportunities and that the state and community had a duty to provide such opportunities. What these committed program directors also believed, however, was that the distinct missions of institutions like HCC and Flagship had implications for instructional quality.

The Mirror Test

Mary Martin was one of these committed program directors, and she would frequently joke at the beginning of each semester that she was about to apply "the mirror test" as she scrambled to staff sections added at the eleventh hour to accommodate unexpected student demand: Mary said she would hire all credentialed instructors who would "fog up a mirror held in front of their face." In short, if they were alive, Mary would hire them. Mary cautioned Henrietta that this was HCC's "dirty little secret." "Yes," Mary acknowledged, "most of us are committed to the ideals of open access and the comprehensive mission, but we know instructional quality suffers because of this. We provide opportunities by scheduling new class sections even when we know they are likely to result in poor student learning."

Henrietta and Mary became friends because their offices were in the same wing of the Jones Classroom Building. But their friendship was tested in Henrietta's second year after a particularly heated debate at the semester's first Academic Council meeting. Mary and other program directors had opened the meeting expressing concern that HCC was sacrificing instructional quality to provide access to as many students as possible. Others responded, however, that the problem was better explained as a lack of organizational skill than inherent conflict between commitments to open access and quality instruction.

The debate turned testy as personal work habits became the focus of attention. The room hushed when Henrietta interjected that she had regularly staffed 60 sections a semester while at Flagship and had never compromised faculty quality. Some veteran program directors turned and looked at Henrietta with wonderment. After prompting from some of her colleagues, Henrietta explained that she had used full-time faculty, adjuncts, and graduate students to staff lower-level undergraduate courses every semester for 12 years at Flagship. And, she added, "I never compromised on quality. It just wasn't an option at our institution."

Developing an Integration Strategy

Henrietta told the group she still had concerns about academic integrity when HCC enrolled students with poor academic skills. She retained her reservations about HCC's emphasis on developing new instructional programs when others could benefit from an increased budget. But after two years at HCC, she said she felt she had developed a committed group of full-time faculty, many of whom were able to pick up an extra section when needed. She also had developed a strong adjunct cadre capable of taking on additional sections on short notice when the need arose. She reported that the English and social science faculty also had identified appropriate content and instructional skills, providing Henrietta with guidance on who would be appropriate faculty for the group's courses. In short, Henrietta had used her leadership skills to develop a solution (tried and tested during her years at Flagship) to maintaining a high-quality faculty and to staffing sections on short notice while maintaining high-quality standards.

As Henrietta sat down, she noticed Mary glaring at her. Henrietta did not acknowledge the glare; she immediately realized that the solution she offered her Academic Council colleagues could be the same solution for the issues she had raised. Challenges to quality teaching and learning posed by underprepared students might be resolved by better leadership and, in this case, better placement and developmental course sequences. Similarly, Henrietta suspected HCC's best occupational program directors might have leadership solutions to starting up new programs while minimizing the budget implications for established programs. Perhaps better industry partnerships or grant funding could help HCC become more successful in starting up new programs while providing a greater share of expansion money to established curricula.

▧ *Analysis of Henrietta's Strategy*

Our vignette offers one account of how a campus leader might harmonize personal values developed during previous work experience and her new college's professional ethics. In this case, Henrietta Higgins found a way to reconcile her commitment to quality instruction with the professional ethics of HCC leaders' commitment to open access and the comprehensive mission.

Henrietta's experience is offered with some caveats. First, it is intended to explain how an integration strategy might evolve without institutional support or mentoring. In the next section, we offer concrete suggestions for institutionalizing the support and mentoring most likely to result in a positive and constructive professional ethical identity. Second, we realize that the challenges facing many institutions may require much more than Henrietta Higgins's drive and talent. Many institutions may be mired in such challenging circumstances that professional ethical identity development for campus leaders is necessary, but not sufficient to establishing a healthy culture committed to the community college's educational principles. Nevertheless, we believe community college leadership initiatives are seldom examined with a view toward promoting professional ethical identity. Our comments below are offered with a view toward meeting this objective.

Formalizing the Process of Developing a Professional Ethical Identity _____

Community college leaders may pursue a variety of options to promote professional ethical identity development. We endorse campus professional development programs as one option for this work and recommend that state leaders incorporate professional ethical identity development in system-wide workshops and leadership academies. Finally, we propose that graduate programs implement professional ethical identity development as an essential discussion topic. When such development is offered in these settings, we contend that its understanding is contingent on the following four components: discussion of the professional ethical identity development literature; self-assessment of existing personal values; student role-plays using problems and issues germane to the individual community college campus or the community college system; and journey mapping to help leaders track their professional ethical identity evolution.

Developing an Integration Strategy in Formalized Learning Activities_____

Because successful incorporation of learning activities concerning professional ethical identity development will require adjustment and revision to any program or curriculum, we decline to propose specific examples here. However, we believe a sound understanding of the four components just identified is essential for learning facilitators responsible for creating appropriate learning activities. Accordingly, we now offer our perspective on these components. In our view, any effort to attend to professional ethical identity development, whether instituted as a part of a campus professional program, state-wide leadership academy, or graduate program, must acknowledge these components.

Literature on Professional Ethical Identity Development

Learning facilitators will be prepared to help community college leaders develop an integration strategy and enhance their professional ethical identity if they are aware of what is known and not known about these constructs: professional ethical identity and psychological acculturation. To begin with, facilitators will need to acknowledge and be able to explain Berry's (1980, 2003) model of acculturation and Handelsman et al.'s (2005) conceptualization of professional ethical identity. These theories provide the foundation for understanding the central principles involved when leaders must identify and reconcile conflicts between their personal values and the college's core principles.

However, it also is important to note that there is little if any empirical research justifying the professional ethical identity theory. We do not see this lack of empirical research as a limitation, but an opportunity for community college leaders to determine how the acculturation theories accommodate their experiences and whether revision to this theory is appropriate. Handelsman et al. approach these concepts as practicing psychologists, and there may be aspects of their discipline, training, and professional experiences that may be especially suitable for understanding professional ethical identity development in terms of successful or unsuccessful strategies. We know community college leaders come to their careers from a wide variety of backgrounds; thus, facilitators focusing on professional ethical identity development will need not only to explain the relevant literature, but they will also need to allow for working revision of the theory to make it coherent for leaders attempting to reconcile a wide range of personal beliefs with their community colleges' unique organizational values.

Self-Assessment of Existing Values

As an essential part of developing an integration strategy to promote a professional ethical identity, we recommend that community college leaders carefully reflect on their existing values and personal code of ethics. To be genuine, this activity needs to be done under the circumstances most likely to result in honest and candid self-assessment. Accordingly, we believe this activity must be conducted without peer oversight and should be completed over a period of days, not hours.

Self-assessing existing values and personal codes should have three elements. First, it should prompt leaders to identify and explain the critical events in their lives as children and as young adults that precipitated development of core personal values and an understanding of right and wrong behavior. Second, this process should ask leaders to record and assess activities in their formal education and training that were instrumental in developing important personal beliefs. Lastly, facilitators should invite leaders to identify and interpret critical events in their professional careers central in developing professional values. Values identified in youth, formal education, and professional careers may form a harmonious network of interrelated beliefs. Then again, introspection may reveal incongruities and perhaps even inconsistencies in personal beliefs about appropriate interactions with others and the nature of professional commitments on the job. What is essential is that leaders understand their personal norms concerning moral behavior as applied to professional relationships and tasks. Only when this understanding exists can leaders begin the process of consciously developing and then monitoring a successful integration strategy.

Student Role-Playing

We believe development of a professional ethical identity and integration strategy is best assured by incorporating student role-plays into programs and curricula. This activity can serve two purposes. It can enable community college leaders to verbalize their attempts to resolve the tension between personal beliefs and organizational values, enabling leaders to help one another when an individual misunderstands the theory, the concepts, or the tension between personal beliefs and organizational values. Next, this activity can provide community college leaders with the peer support and validation needed to carry out the kind of honest and candid self-assessment that will help identify deep-seated personal values.

Community college leaders must frequently respond to demanding campus needs; often they are called on to solve complex problems involving a variety of concerns under trying circumstances. When the pressure of the moment forces leaders to solve problems without factoring in their personal beliefs or the fundamental values of the organization, no one is well served. Student role-plays can assist leaders in developing a practice that acknowledges and accommodates their personal beliefs and the college's professional values.

Journey Mapping

To help leaders understand the evolution of their professional ethical identity, we recommend facilitators invite community college leaders to record their observations and interpretation of critical events as a part of a regular journaling activity. Seasoned leaders know journaling can provide important insights into changes concerning their personal goals, ambitions, strengths, and weaknesses. It can also help leaders attain a better sense of how their professional ethical identities may be evolving along with changes in their professional and personal lives. Individual leaders may conclude this evolution is positive or negative. Journey mapping provides a mechanism to remain aware of such changes so that leaders can adjust their course when necessary.

At the end of the day, community college leaders must be able to integrate their personal values with the fundamental values of the community college. This integration will help ensure that public two-year institutions are served by a leadership cadre not only prepared to maintain the principles of community college education, but also prepared to work toward refining these principles to develop stronger and better colleges for the future.

Conclusion

Community college leaders will face new challenges that call for a sound professional ethical identity. Using the work of Berry (1980, 2003), Berry and Sam (1997), and Handelsman et al. (2005), we have articulated an acculturation model to facilitate professional ethical identity development in community college leaders. We agree with Handelsman et al. that the integration strategy promotes one's professional ethical identity, whereas the other three strategies may result in misuses of personal ethics codes or alienation from the organization and profession. Lastly, we believe the integration strategy may be affirmed by education and training incorporated into formal training in graduate programs, professional development programs, and possibly even professional training workshops.

We build on this chapter in Chapter 14, "The Consequences of Compromised Ethical Identity Development in Community College Leadership." Specifically, we use three vignettes to describe and explain adverse strategies that reflect an inappropriate balance between personal ethics of origin and the organizational values for community college leaders, and we propose an organizational process for assisting leaders in developing an integration strategy that promotes respect for personal ethics of origin and the critical values of community college education.

References

Amey, M. J., VanDerLinden, K. E., & Brown, D. F. (2002, August). Perspectives on community college leadership: Twenty years in the making. *Community College Journal of Research and Practice, 26*(7/8), 573–589.

Anderson, P., Murray, J. P., & Olivarez, A., Jr. (2002, Fall). The managerial roles of public community college chief academic officers. *Community College Review, 30*(2), 1–26.

Anderson, S. K., & Davies, T. G. (2000, October). An ethical decision-making model: A necessary tool for community college presidents and their boards of trustees. *Community College Journal of Research and Practice, 24*(9), 711–727.

Anderson, S. K., Wagoner, H. T., & Moore, G. K. (2006). Ethical choice: An outcome of being, becoming and doing. In P. Williams & S. K. Anderson, *Law and ethics in coaching: How to solve and avoid difficult problems in your practice* (pp. 39–61). Hoboken, NJ: John Wiley & Sons.

Baker, G. A. (1992). Creative cultures: Towards a new paradigm. In G. A. Baker, *Cultural leadership: Inside America's community colleges* (pp. 1–16). Washington, DC: Community College Press.

Baker, G. A. (2002, August). American higher education at the Rubicon: A partnership for progress. *Community College Journal of Research and Practice, 26*(7/8), 629–644.

Berry, J. W. (1980). Acculturation as varieties of adaptation. In A. M. Padilla (Ed.), *Acculturation: Theory, models, and some new findings* (pp. 9–25). Boulder, CO: Westview Press.

Berry, J. W. (2003). Conceptual approaches to acculturation. In K. M. Chun, P. B. Organista, & G. Marin (Eds.), *Acculturation: Advances in theory, measurement, and applied research* (pp. 17–37). Washington, DC: American Psychological Association.

Berry, J. W., & Sam, D. L. (1997). Acculturation and adaptation. In J. W. Berry, M. H. Segall, & C. Kagitcibasi (Eds.), *Handbook of cross-cultural psychology: Vol. 3. Social behaviour and applications* (2nd ed., pp. 291–326). Boston, MA: Allyn & Bacon.

Brown, L., Martinez, M., & Daniel, D. (2002, Summer). Community college leadership preparation: Needs, perceptions, and recommendations. *Community College Review, 30*(1), 45–73.

Davies, T. G., & Quick, D. (2001, September). Reducing distance through distance learning: The community college leadership doctoral program at Colorado State University. *Community College Journal of Research and Practice, 25*(8), 607–620.

Handelsman, M. M., Gottlieb, M. C., & Knapp, S. (2005, February). Training ethical psychologists: An acculturation model. *Professional Psychology: Research and Practice, 36*(1), 59–65.

Harbour, C., & Nagy, P. (2005, July). Assessing a state-mandated institutional accountability program: The perceptions of selected community college leaders. *Community College Journal of Research and Practice, 29*(6), 445–461.

Lovell, N., Crittenden, L., Stumpf, D., & Davis, M. (2003, January). The road less traveled: Atypical doctoral preparation of leaders in rural community colleges. *Community College Journal of Research and Practice, 27*(1), 1–14.

McArthur, R. C. (2002, Winter). Democratic leadership and faculty empowerment at the community college: A theoretical model for the department chair. *Community College Review, 30*(3), 1–11.

Miller, M. T., & Pope, M. L. (2003, February). Faculty senate leadership as a presidential pathway: Clear passage or caught in a maze? *Community College Journal of Research and Practice, 27*(2), 119–130.

Townsend, B. K., & Bassoppo-Moyo, S. (1997, Fall). The effective community college academic administrator: Necessary competencies and attitudes. *Community College Review, 25*(2), 41–56.

Vaughan, G. B. (1992). *Dilemmas of leadership: Decision making and ethics in the community college.* San Francisco, CA: Jossey-Bass.

Part II

Daily Practice of Ethical Leadership

Chapter 7   Ethical Leadership: A Faculty Obligation
Beth Richardson-Mitchell

Chapter 8   The Interface of Ethics and Courage
in the Life of a Chief Academic Officer
Linda Lucas

Chapter 9   Threats to Ethical Leadership: The Hubris
of Absolutism, the Politics of Affinity-Based
Decision-Making, and the Development of
Unethical Followers
David E. Hardy

Chapter 10   Leading From the Head and the Heart
Susan K. Chappell

Chapter 11   Transformational Leadership and Ethical
Dilemmas in Community Colleges
Sherry Stout-Stewart

Chapter 12   Presidential Support for Civic Engagement
and Leadership Education
Louis S. Albert

Chapter 13   A Guide to Ethical Decision-Making by
Presidents and Boards
Gary W. Davis

Chapter 14   The Consequences of Compromised
Ethical Identity Development in
Community College Leadership
*Clifford P. Harbour, Sharon K. Anderson,
Timothy Gray Davies*

7

Ethical Leadership: A Faculty Obligation

Beth Richardson-Mitchell

> *A vision is a target that beckons.*
> —Warren Bennis and Burt Nanus

Each morning, as I walk down the hall to my office on the main campus of Mayland Community College in North Carolina, I reflect on my vision as an educator and a leader. I focus on my responsibilities for teaching the subjects of communication and humanities; for coordinating Mayland's student orientation program; for advising students as they progress toward their personal and professional goals; and, ultimately, for facilitating the growth of the "whole person" in each student who crosses my path. I want to fulfill these responsibilities with the highest levels of quality and care. I realize, however, that the last of these responsibilities, facilitating the growth of the whole person, can be especially challenging. One approach to consider in this endeavor consists of three actions: communicating to students what it means to be a whole person; practicing ethical leadership; and engaging students in character development exercises.

Communicate to Students What It Means To Be a Whole Person _____

How can one define the whole person? Greek philosopher Aristotle provides a start with the concept of *ethos*, which refers to one's character, that is, one's credibility or trustworthiness (Kies, 2007). Though mainly used in the study and practice of rhetoric, ethos is a powerful concept to consider in personal development. According to Thomas Rivers (2004), "the art of rhetoric is the oldest of our disciplines that self-consciously and systematically has placed character education at its center" (p. 247). Richard Hersh and Carol Schneider (2005) state, "For institutions that seek to educate the 'whole person,' the challenge of educating for personal and social responsibility has taken on new urgency" (p. 6). They further purport the following:

> Personal responsibility and social responsibility involve the moral obligation to both self and community, and both forms of responsibility rely upon such virtues as honesty, self-discipline, respect, loyalty, and compassion. The formation of these personal and social dispositions is powerfully influenced by the character of the community culture, and the community's own integrity and vitality depends, in turn, on the values, actions, and contributions of its members. (p. 8)

The Dalai Lama (1999) complements this idea:

> To develop a sense of universal responsibility—of the universal dimension of our every act and of the equal right of all others to happiness and not to suffer—is to develop an attitude of mind whereby when we see an opportunity to benefit others, we will take it in preference to merely looking after our own narrow interests. (pp. 162–163)

The whole person is one who understands that "leadership is everyone's vocation, and it can be an evasion to insist that it is not. When we live in the close-knit ecosystem called community, everyone follows and everyone leads" (Palmer, 2000, p. 74).

One can also incorporate a creator mentality, described by Skip Downing (2005) as one in which "people change their beliefs and behaviors to create the best results they can" (p. 26). According to Downing, everyone has a choice regarding every stimulus he or she encounters; the creator chooses to seek solutions, take action, and try something new. As a result, he or she often achieves his or her goals. In contrast to the creator, a victim chooses to blame, complain, excuse, and repeat ineffective behavior; he or she seldom achieves his or her goals. Rivers (2004) asserts that one may not choose his or her personality, but one does choose his or her character.

As a faculty member, it is my ethical obligation to share with students what I perceive constitutes the whole person. This is a logical first step in helping them choose and/or develop their character; however, simply conveying this information is not enough. For students to take their task seriously, they must see that I personally strive to reach high levels of character and "embrace the role of mentor, opening up . . . storehouses of knowledge [and experiences] . . . and inviting them to enter" (Stillion & Siegel, 1994, p. 70).

Practice Ethical Leadership

As a role model and mentor, I am a leader. As a leader of character, it is imperative that I adhere to ethical behaviors and attitudes in the classroom and the community at large. What might be some significant leadership considerations? Max DePree (1992) affirms that leaders should be successful and faithful in "the active pursuit of a common good" (p. 9). He suggests five criteria for entering the realm of faithfulness (pp. 10–12):

- *Integrity in all things* precedes all else. . . . Leaders understand the profound difference between gestures and commitment.

- *The servanthood of leadership* needs to be felt, understood, believed, and practiced if we're to be faithful.

- *Accountability for others,* especially those on the edges of life and not yet experienced in the ways of the world. . . . Leaders should encourage and sustain those on the bottom rung first.

- *The practice of equity.* . . . While equity should certainly guide the apportioning of resources, it is far more important in our human relationships.

- Leaders have to be *vulnerable,* have to offer others the opportunity to do their best. Leaders become vulnerable by sharing with others the marvelous gift of being personally accountable.

Even though DePree focuses on leadership in the context of business, his criteria for faithfulness are applicable to higher education. To sum up the idea of integrity, the statement "Say what you mean, and mean what you say" is apropos. Students value instructors who are true to their word, in knowledge as well as in deed.

Tapping into DePree's second criterion, the servanthood of leadership, I believe Lao Tzu provides key words of wisdom: "To lead, one must follow." Students know when faculty strive to serve and have others' best interests at heart. I have been fortunate to work at a college where accountability for others is valued very highly. It is my calling to "strike a careful balance between support and challenge" (McGonigal, 2005, p. 2); I must inspire students at all levels to do well, to provide strategies and resources to assist and empower.

The practice of equity, DePree's fourth criterion, is very much like mutual respect. Faculty should interact with students as fellow human beings, leaving aside issues of "control" or "position." In lieu of ego, faculty should focus on helping students discover their strengths; providing diplomatic, constructive feedback to assist students as they improve their skills; and, lastly, understanding and communicating that each student has value.

The last criterion, being vulnerable, means the leader can "let go" and delegate more tasks to his or her followers. The leader empowers followers to be more responsible and "in charge." Working with students so they are "personally accountable" (DePree, 1992, p. 12) is a main goal of faculty. Providing students with the necessary content knowledge, clear instructions, and moral support allows more opportunities for them to "step up to the plate" and achieve their objectives as active learners.

In addition to DePree's criteria for faithfulness in leadership, one can also study and exercise five fundamental practices of exemplary leadership detailed by James Kouzes and Barry Posner (1995, pp. 8–13):

- Challenging the process. . . . Leaders are early *adopters* of innovation. Leaders know well that experimentation, innovation, and change all involve risk and failure, but they proceed anyway.

- Inspiring a shared vision. . . . [Leaders] gaze across the horizon of time, imagining the attractive opportunities that are in store when they and their constituents arrive at a distant destination.

- Enabling others to act. . . . Leadership is a team effort. . . . Exemplary leaders enlist the support and assistance of all those who must make the project work.

- Modeling the way. . . . Titles are granted, but it's your behavior that wins you respect. . . . Leaders go first. They set an example and build commitment through simple, daily acts that create progress and momentum. Leaders model the way through personal example and dedicated execution.

- Encouraging the heart. . . . People become exhausted, frustrated, and disenchanted. They're often tempted to give up. *Leaders encourage the heart of their constituents to carry on.*

These five fundamental practices have their roots in business but lend themselves well to academe.

As a faculty member, I admire instructors and administrators who challenge the process, the first of the five practices of exemplary leadership. They have inspired me to try new, potentially more effective teaching strategies and methods of assessment characteristic of learning colleges. Living in the digital age as all educators do, it is also imperative to discover and apply new technologies, both in the seated classroom and online (Richardson, 1998). What if I try to do something new, something better, and it does not work well? "Failure is an important teacher in the transformational process," argues Robert Quinn. "If you learn from it and go on experimenting, you become more unique; you gain the power to help people transform their lives" (Quinn & Anding, 2005, p. 493).

Shared vision, the second practice, is essential in learning. Faculty must be very clear about their intended outcomes for classes (and advising outside of the classroom). Many miscommunications and frustrations brew when outcomes are difficult to identify and convey. Students must be on solid ground in order for them to develop confidence in learning and achieving their goals. Stillion and Siegel (1994) sum up this idea eloquently:

> Planning and organization of classes become extremely important teaching activities and the faculty member gradually comes to view himself or herself as the director of a symphony, in which every student is a musician who must be encouraged to develop expertise in using his/her instrument, the mind, to its fullest. (p. 70)

Enabling others to act, Kouzes and Posner's third practice, is integral to learner-centered instruction. As the saying goes, "Be a guide on the side instead of a sage on stage." Students learn more when they are active participants, especially when they can directly apply or teach the material themselves. To be most successful with higher, more involved learning, students need faculty who model the way, faculty who engage in the fourth practice of exemplary leadership. A faculty member engaging in virtuous behaviors and attitudes, a faculty member who demonstrates ethos—character, trustworthiness, and credibility—will inspire students to make wise decisions and become more personally and socially responsible.

Poet e. e. cummings's famous line, "i carry your heart (i carry it in my heart)," captures the essence of the final practice of exemplary leadership, encouraging the heart. Students who know their teachers care tend to "hang in there" when times get tough. Faculty treating students as human beings, not machines, make the difference. In my communication classes, I ask students what helps them feel valued by faculty. Time and again, they share the following: meaningful feedback in class and on written assignments; words of support; and positive, caring tone of voice, facial expressions, and eye contact.

Engage Students in Character Development Exercises

In addition to teaching the attributes of the whole person and being an effective role model, mentor, and leader, one can introduce relatively simple ways students can practice being individuals of high character, creating what Quinn calls "deep change" (Quinn & Anding, 2005, p. 489). He states, "Unless work is done to the contrary, all living systems move toward entropy or the loss of productive energy" (p. 489).

Skip Downing, who conceptualized the creator versus victim mentality, authored a textbook and conducts training on what many of my faculty colleagues consider the development of the whole person. Students in college orientation and advising programs across the nation have used Downing's text, *On Course: Strategies for Creating Success in College and in Life* (2005), and have made measurable progress in terms of personal responsibility, self-motivation, self-management, independence, self-awareness, lifelong learning, emotional intelligence, and belief in themselves. One of many strategies Downing introduces, the Wise-Choice Process, empowers students to exercise personal responsibility and make good decisions by answering six questions:

- What's my present situation?
- What would I like my situation to be?
- Do I have a choice here?
- What are my possible choices?
- What's the likely outcome of each possible choice?
- Which choice(s) will I commit to doing? (pp. 35–37)

The following is an example of a typical student response to the Wise-Choice Process:

- What's my present situation? I am not doing well in my English class. I'm not even sure if I'm passing. I don't know what to do.

- What would I like my situation to be? At this point, I would be really happy to earn a B or C in English.

- Do I have a choice here? Skip Downing says I always have a choice. My issue is if I'll make the right one.

- What are my possible choices? Well, I can talk with my instructor to see exactly where I stand and ask what I can do to improve my writing skills. I can go to the counseling center and sign up for a tutor. Maybe I can schedule time to sit down with Mom, who can teach me what she knows about grammar. I can go online to find a prewritten paper that will earn me an A if I don't get caught. This is so hard. I may just quit. All this is too much trouble.

- What's the likely outcome of each possible choice? My instructor seems okay. I think she would let me know how I'm doing. A friend from class is meeting with her during office hours for help, and he's doing better. The counseling center, if a tutor is available, would be great! I need to check and see if the service is free. Mom knows her stuff, but she might be too busy since she's working and taking care of my little brother and sister. A couple of people in my last English class tried to download papers and pass them off as their own; they were busted and failed the class because the instructor Googled some of the sentences in the papers. This wouldn't be any good. If I quit this class, I will need to take it sometime. What if I quit school altogether? There's no way I could get the job I want.

• Which choice(s) will I commit to doing? I know that whatever I commit to I really have to follow through with it. I'm going to make an appointment with my instructor during her office hours to get help. Heck, maybe my friend and I could meet with her at the same time. I'll also see if there is a tutor available to review my writing with me.

This is a rather typical scenario at my college. Other challenges include getting to campus in time for classes, ensuring assignments are being done correctly, having enough money to stay in college, and dealing with stressful relationships. The Wise-Choice questions are rather basic, but they are thought provoking and encourage students to generate positive commitments on their own instead of passively deferring to what others tell them to do or possibly giving up after concluding that they have no alternatives.

Shanks (1997) offers another way for students to develop their character and thereby engage in personally and socially responsible behavior on a regular basis. This option, Shanks' Five Questions: A Systemic Approach, is as follows:

• Did I practice any virtues today?

• Did I do more good than harm today?

• Did I treat people with dignity and respect today?

• Was I fair and just today?

• Was my community better because I was in it? Was I better because I was in my community? (pp. 2–3)

Students using this option engage in meaningful thought when they process these questions. Observe the first question, for example: "Did I practice any virtues today?" To respond, students need to know what virtues are. Shanks (1997) states that virtues "are the best parts of ourselves" (pp. 2–3). Do students consider themselves honest, compassionate, dedicated, and/or respectful? When students address the second question, what do they consider, in general, to be good compared to harm? Did their judgment in a particular situation seem reasonable? Did they do their best to accomplish what they believe is for the common good? The third question focuses on dignity and respect. Shanks's perspective on this question is compelling:

> All human beings should be treated with dignity simply
> because they are human. People have moral rights, espe-
> cially the fundamental right to be treated as free and equal
> human beings, not as things to be manipulated, con-
> trolled, or cast away. (p. 3)

Do students step back and reflect on how they really communicate with
others as human beings of value? Do they adhere to the Golden Rule?

The fourth question, about fairness and justice, relates to equality. If
students do not treat others with equality, why not? Do they have any ethically sound reasons to justify their actions? Shanks's final question, relating to the interdependence of students and their community, is
significant. The ideal, according to Shanks, is for the community to be a
better place based on students reaching out beyond themselves and for the
students to be better people as a result of the community's influence. Do
students participate in community service, student government, church,
and/or other extracurricular pursuits that will improve their communities
and themselves?

Conclusion

The responsibilities of faculty, from effectively instructing their disciplines
to facilitating the growth of the whole person in their students, are critical.
Consider the words of Marvin W. Berkowitz as cited by Hersh and Schneider (2005): "Education inevitably affects character, either intentionally or
unintentionally" (p. 9). Faculty must be ethical leaders with a vision to affect character intentionally.

References

DePree, M. (1992). *Leadership jazz.* New York, NY: Dell.

Downing, S. (2005). *On course: Strategies for creating success in college and
    in life.* Boston, MA: Houghton Mifflin.

Hersh, R. H., & Schneider, C. G. (2005, Summer/Fall). Fostering per-
    sonal and social responsibility on college and university campuses.
    Liberal Education, 91(3/4), 6.

Kies, D. (2007). *Ethical appeal: Ethos.* Retrieved August 21, 2006, from papyr.com/hypertextbooks/comp1/ethos.htm

Kouzes, J. M., & Posner, B. Z. (1995). *The leadership challenge: How to keep getting extraordinary things done in organizations.* San Francisco, CA: Jossey-Bass.

Lama, D. (1999). *Ethics for the new millennium.* New York, NY: Riverhead Books.

McGonigal, K. (2005). Teaching for transformation: From learning theory to teaching strategies. *Speaking of Teaching, 14*(2), 1–4.

Palmer, P. J. (2000). *Let your life speak: Listening for the voice of vocation.* San Francisco, CA: Jossey-Bass.

Quinn, R. E., & Anding, J. M. (2005). An interview with Robert E. Quinn. Entering the fundamental state of leadership: Reflections on the path to transformational teaching. *Academy of Management Learning and Education, 4*(4), 487–495.

Richardson, B. (1998, December). Seven practices to prepare our students for success in the digital age. *Leadership Abstracts, 11*(10). Retrieved December 1, 2006, from www.league.org/publication /abstracts /leadership/labs1298.htm

Rivers, T. M. (2004). Ten essentials for character education. *Journal of General Education, 53*(3–4), 247–260.

Shanks, T. (1997, Winter). Everyday ethics. *Issues in Ethics,* 8(1). Retrieved December 1, 2006, from www.scu.edu/ethics/publications/iie /v8n1/everydayethics.html

Stillion, J. M., & Siegel, B. L. (1994, Summer). The transformational college teacher. *Journal of Invitational Theory and Practice, 3*(2), 55–74.

8

The Interface of Ethics
and Courage in the Life
of a Chief Academic Officer

Linda Lucas

Although I attended an excellent university, there was no course in ethics in my graduate program. The topic was addressed quite thoroughly, however, in a course in which I developed a working philosophy of adult education. I was required to explore systematically my beliefs and values about teaching and learning and the role of an administrator in that process, make underlying assumptions and tacit beliefs explicit, and come to conclusions about what was right and true and efficacious, at least from my point of view. I learned the lesson that this solid philosophical foundation would promote consistency in thought and action and lead to effective professional practice. The work I did in this course 25 years ago has served me well in the different positions I have held in higher education.

As I reviewed my ethical framework for the purposes of this chapter, it occurred to me that I could organize my ethical framework into three main groups: *professional ethics,* the broadest and deepest beliefs and values I hold about the profession of education; *personal ethics,* how I define who I am as a person in an ethical sense; and *situational ethics,* the roles and responsibilities of a particular position I hold at any point in time.

When I consider the beliefs and values concerning the profession of education and who I am as a professional in that field, which I developed in that adult education course long ago, what comes to mind initially are thoughts related to human nature. I believe that, broadly speaking, the project of one's education is to become more fully human, and that if people are fortunate enough to live in nurturing and benign conditions, they are naturally curious, want to engage with their environment, and are intrinsically motivated to learn. Carl Rogers (1978) has referred to a formative, directional tendency in human beings that leads them to increasingly complex levels of engagement with the world around them. If this state of being is in fact our natural birthright, or the essence of what it means to be human, then it follows that learning and curiosity are a part of the life force and as such are both powerful and sacred. Conversely, erecting barriers against this life force is immoral.

These lofty philosophical thoughts have both theoretical and practical implications for professional practice in higher education. They ground my beliefs about teaching and learning and my role as an administrator in the following ways: Teachers should honor their profession, act with integrity, encourage integrity in their students, honor their students' capacity to learn in different ways, treat their students with respect, nurture learning, and identify and remove barriers that work against learning. Learners have the right to be treated with respect, to learn in their own style, to have reasonable accommodations made for them if necessary, and to make choices that direct the course and content of their learning. They have the right to receive access to a high-quality curriculum and good teaching, which will help them to develop their capacities and talents and thus contribute to the world around them. My role as an administrator is to support faculty and learners in this endeavor in multiple ways in order to create an environment in which learning will flourish.

While professional ethics form the foundation of my professional identity, personal ethics form the foundation of who I am as a person. These are the ethics I carry with me wherever I go, regardless of professional or situational variables. My personal ethical framework, and thus my sense of personal wholeness, rests on the principles of authenticity, fairness, honesty, and respect for self and others.

Authenticity means being true to my deepest self regardless of pressures that may work against that. It means taking pride in setting and meeting my own standards of behavior, or at least attempting to do so. It means having the courage of my convictions and accepting responsibility for my decisions and actions.

Fairness means playing by commonly understood rules and not changing those rules arbitrarily or capriciously to serve my interests or the interests of my friends. It means not using or withholding information to manipulate other people. It means seeking out and examining all available information before coming to a decision.

Honesty is required with other people and with myself, particularly in terms of acknowledging my faults and shortcomings and not projecting them onto others. Honesty means that I try to see situations as clearly as possible, remaining open to information that I may find frightening or difficult to accept.

Showing *respect for myself and others* is reflected in listening and trying to empathize with the feelings and thoughts of others, honoring personal and professional boundaries and multiple points of view, and being sensitive to the impact of my actions on others.

Situational ethics pertains to my specific position and its attendant duties; it requires that I adhere to college policies and procedures and that I use the power vested in my position not for personal gain but to perform supervisory and academic leadership responsibilities in a manner that serves students and promotes the mission of the college.

When I think of ethics, I think of integrity, which is the observance of ethical principles and the state of being uncorrupted. From my point of view, these two definitions are two sides of the same coin—that is, in order to remain uncorrupted, one must adhere to one's ethical principles. Professional ethics, personal ethics, and situational ethics interact dynamically. If there is congruence within each of these dimensions and across all three, my integrity and sense of wholeness remain intact. If there is incongruence within a dimension or across the dimensions, I am conscious of dissonance, which is more or less distressing, depending on the situation.

Scenarios Involving Ethics_____

The subject of ethics has been debated for more than 2,000 years, and the typical chief academic officer is unlikely to have a broad and deep understanding of this scholarly tradition. However, since a chief academic officer is confronted daily with situations that require ethical decisions, he or she needs a working philosophy of ethics, similar to the working philosophy of education described earlier. The words can be changed slightly, but the process and the intent are the same: to develop an ethical/philosophical foundation that promotes consistency in thought and action and leads to effective professional practice.

Keeping in mind the above-stated beliefs as a foundation, when an ethical dilemma emerges, I follow a theory-in-use approach that involves the consideration of a number of criteria as well as a process of information gathering and decision-making. My criteria for decision-making include the following: What is fair? What is rational? Who or what is the most important thing in this situation? What is the right thing to do? Has all available information been considered? What are the ramifications of various decisions that could be made? Will I be able to defend this decision publicly and with a clear conscience, if that becomes necessary?

To gain an understanding of the situation from multiple viewpoints, I gather information from people and other resources. I reflect on this information and, sometimes alone and sometimes with others, craft a decision that takes into account all available information and meets ethical criteria. I then follow through with any necessary actions.

Scenario 1: Anna's Grade

Anna is an adult, nontraditional student who performs well academically. As she nears completion of her program, she contacts me about an F grade she received almost a year ago. She tells me that during the semester in which she earned this grade, her young child died of a protracted and painful disease. Anna tried to discuss the situation with her instructor at the time, but the instructor was unsympathetic and unresponsive. Anna admits that she may not have followed college policy about withdrawing from a course because of the grief and disarray she and her family were experiencing. Anna requests that the grade be removed from her transcript and strengthens her request by stating that the course in question was not required for her program and that she subsequently took and did well in a higher-level course.

College policy clearly states deadlines for withdrawing from courses and clearly states that while amelioration policies exist, no course and grade may be totally expunged from a transcript. According to this policy, Anna's request could not be granted. The issue is this: Must college policy be followed, or should an exception to policy be granted? I was very sympathetic to Anna, and I wanted to change her grade.

Could I find a way to change her grade that would honor college policy, be fair to other students, and stand up to public scrutiny in the unlikely event that there were any? Was there any lapse on the part of the college in terms of teaching, advising, or communication with Anna that could be used as a rationale for granting her request? Granting a grade change based solely on compassion for Anna would lead to an unacceptable situation in which other students might be required to meet a similar standard in order to get a similar decision. What would be as legitimate? Anna's situation, as heartbreaking as it was, was not a sufficient foundation on which to base a decision.

I reviewed Anna's transcript and consulted with people who had knowledge of Anna and her situation to get their points of view. I considered Anna's exemplary academic record, her concern about having the F on her transcript, and the recommendations of two faculty members who spoke on her behalf. I was informed that Anna's instructor, no longer at the college, had had a number of problems with students and was not viewed positively by faculty or staff. Since requests for grade changes usually originate from the instructor, a key fact was that an attempt to reach this instructor to get his input was unsuccessful. I was not able to determine whether he would agree to a change of grade.

After consideration of all of the above, I decided that while the course could not be expunged from the transcript, it was appropriate to change the grade to a "W."

Scenario 2: Review of the Math Curriculum

Because of concerns expressed by a number of faculty about the content and sequencing of several math courses, I decided that the math curriculum needed to be reviewed. In order to make changes that could go into effect in a timely way, a window of only three months was available to study issues, make recommendations, and put these recommendations through appropriate curriculum review bodies. Knowing that the math faculty were busy teaching courses and carrying out other duties, I hired an external consultant and directed her to survey appropriate people and groups, write a report, and make recommendations that would be studied by math faculty and other interested parties. I directed the consultant to get input from math faculty regarding whom to survey and what to ask.

I explained to faculty that the consultant had been hired only to speed up the process and that the intention was not to criticize their performance or the curriculum. Rather, the purpose was to explore concerns presented to me, and, if possible, identify changes that would benefit students. The math faculty reluctantly went along with the project. Within a very short time, the consultant completed her work and wrote an excellent report. Information in the report reinforced and succinctly stated concerns that had been expressed by a number of people, including faculty, for a number of years.

The report was submitted to the chief academic office, a copy was given to the chair of the math department, and I made it known that the report was available for review in my office. Unfortunately, some faculty and staff had made critical and even mean-spirited comments about the math faculty and curriculum, and the math faculty were enraged by the report. A blame-storm ensued, directed toward the CAO, in which I was vehemently criticized for hiring a consultant to do what the math faculty said they were capable of doing. I was also criticized for making the report available for review.

On a more positive note, discussion about the report resulted in several changes that greatly benefited students. A new math course expected to enhance student success and retention was designed for one program. Other changes made it possible for students in another program to finish in the customary two-year period even if they needed remedial work, whereas previously such students were forced to stay in school for two-and-a-half or even three years to complete all requirements. A spillover effect of the math discussion was that several courses in the science department were also revised, resulting in improved and streamlined curriculum for students and decreased scheduling problems for the college. A final benefit was that faculty from multiple departments collaborated very productively on the project.

In reflecting on this scenario, I see a number of questions and issues emerging. One, who is in charge of the curriculum? The president has authority over all curricular matters, taking under advisement recommendations from the chief academic officer and the faculty. Two, math faculty felt that their authority in the curriculum review process had been diminished by the hiring of an external consultant. Three, what about the process and policy for curricular review? All programs and departments are reviewed on a five-year cycle according to established processes, and math faculty felt that this process was circumvented by the review that was done. Finally, making available a report that had critical comments about the math faculty was seen by some as inappropriate.

As I reviewed the fallout from this situation, I considered the following. I hired the consultant because I knew faculty would not have time to do this review. I requested that faculty work with the consultant and be involved during the entire project. If I were doing it again, I would have communicated with the faculty much more clearly that I understood that they had the expertise to conduct a review and that the consultant was hired to help them by doing the legwork and gathering information for the review. I would have gotten a verbal commitment and understanding from the faculty that the consultant was serving the faculty and students, not the chief academic officer.

The college has policies regarding program and curricular review, and I pushed against those policies, specifically in terms of the time frame and haste of the review. My rationale for doing this, as stated earlier, was that there was only a three-month window in which to do the review and make changes that could go into effect during the following year at the earliest. I believed that this haste and pressure were justified because of the concerns expressed to me by faculty and because of the benefits to students that would result if well-thought-out changes were implemented.

I continue to mull over the issue of the negative comments in the report. I could have deleted them, but I am uneasy with this option. In one sense, it insults the intelligence and integrity of the faculty by assuming they are not able to deal with negative feedback and evaluate it for its truth and utility. I also believe there are lessons to be learned about the importance of providing critical feedback with civility and courtesy.

Regarding the availability of the report, my opinion is that openness and honesty contribute to an environment of critical inquiry. Making a report available only to a select group of people contravenes the notion of open communication. And, since faculty outside the math department had expressed concern to me about the issues, it did not seem appropriate to deny them access to the report. In fact, very few people came to my office to read the report.

I continue to reflect on this scenario. Great value came out of the curriculum review, but wounds were inflicted that may not heal for a long time to come. Does the benefit to the students outweigh the fact that collegial relationships may have been damaged? Was the benefit to students worth the wounds that were inflicted?

Scenario 3: Richard and the Required Course

When Richard called me in the middle of spring semester, he was angry. Although he had planned to complete his program in May, his advisor had informed him at his graduation review that he still needed to take a course that was required of all students. This requirement meant that he would not be able to graduate and that he would have to take the course during the summer, which would cost him time and money. Richard had tried earlier to get a waiver for this course because he believed it would repeat prior coursework he had completed at another college. Richard said he would have taken the course in the spring semester, but someone had told him that a waiver would be given, and so he did not register for it. He had no documentation and could not tell me who had given him this information. Regardless, he wanted me to grant the waiver.

One issue here involves the responsibility of the college to advise students appropriately. What was Richard told, by whom, and when? Another issue concerns Richard's responsibility to seek out and act on information that he receives. A final issue concerns whether the course requirement is really justified. Would Richard truly benefit from taking this course, or be harmed by not taking it? What decision would be most beneficial to Richard—to require him to take the course or to release him from that requirement?

The college curriculum is approved by the faculty, and the faculty agreed long ago that this course was a requirement for graduation. Policy states that department chairs must review requests for waivers and may approve or deny them. Their decisions can be overridden by the chief academic officer, but such overrides happen rarely.

The registrar, who does the initial review of all transfer courses, told me that the course Richard wanted to transfer in had never been accepted as a substitute for our required course. I spoke to the department chair, who told me that he had denied the waiver because the course Richard had taken did not include an extensive writing assignment similar in scope to the one in our course. I spoke to Richard's advisor, who told me that Richard was aware of the requirement and chose not to register for the course.

Granting a waiver to Richard under these circumstances would violate college policy, create tension between the department chair and the chief academic officer, and open the door to similar requests from other students. It sounded like an open-and-shut case, yet I had some problems with the course under discussion. I questioned the requirement that all students take it, because I was not convinced that the course was of value to all students or of more value than another course they might take if this requirement were dropped. A similar concern was expressed by some faculty. I also thought that Richard's previous coursework was adequate in this particular instance. Even though there was some indication that he was trying to "work the system," I was uncomfortable with the idea of requiring him to delay graduation and take a course over the summer when I was not sure he would benefit in the short or long term from taking the course. I thought much of it would, in fact, be repetitious and that it would waste his money and his time, which might be more profitably spent learning something else. Holding him to the requirement seemed to serve college policy more than it served Richard.

My decision in this case, made reluctantly, was to adhere to college policy. The harshness of the "sentence" was ameliorated slightly by the fact that Richard would be able to take the course online, which would allow him greater flexibility and would eliminate travel and schedule concerns over the summer. He would also be able to participate in graduation with his fellow students.

Adhering to college policy is always safe. Decisions made on that basis can be demonstrated to be fair and rational and can be made public with relatively little controversy or criticism. Yet, in this particular case, I felt that I did not serve Richard well. In retrospect, I feel I should have opened a discussion with faculty about the value and utility of this course for all students. I did not because I knew it would be an extremely contentious debate. There were numerous other debates already occurring, and I made a strategic decision not to debate the merits of this particular course at that point in time. In any event, a resolution of the issue would have occurred too late to help Richard. I continue to feel that I did not serve Richard well, and I regret that Richard was required to take a course that was of questionable value to him.

Congruence . . . or Lack Thereof _____

Regarding the above scenarios, in determining whether there was congruence both within and across the dimensions of professional, personal, and situational ethics, I need to ask the questions: Did I adhere to my beliefs within each dimension, and were my actions consistent with them? Was there congruence across the three dimensions?

Regarding Anna's grade, professional, personal, and situational dimensions were in alignment. There was congruence within and across dimensions, and I experienced no dissonance. My professional and personal beliefs and values were in alignment with the decision about Anna, and college policy supported the decision as well.

The math curriculum review is more complicated. I acted in a way that was consistent with my beliefs in the professional dimension—in particular, that teachers should identify and remove barriers to learning, that learners have a right to receive access to a high-quality curriculum, and that my responsibility is to create an environment in which learning will flourish.

In the personal dimension, I believed that I showed respect for others, was sensitive to the impact of my actions on them, and was sensitive to boundaries. I acted in a way that I thought was ethical, though others would disagree. Because of the difference between my perception and theirs and because of the fact that I continue to be troubled by their distress, there is dissonance within my personal ethical dimension regarding the math review.

Regarding the situational dimension of the math review, I initiated the review to serve students and the college. I had the authority to do this review and was backed up by the president. Although faculty did not participate greatly, the process was designed to be inclusive. Conversely, the position taken by the faculty was that the normal channels for curriculum review were not followed. While my behavior was consistent with my stated ethical beliefs and values, the perception was that I had acted inappropriately. Thus, there is dissonance within this dimension as well.

The math review had internal dissonance within both personal and situational dimensions of my ethical framework. Given this, dissonance had to exist between these two dimensions and the professional dimension. Thus, the math review had dissonance both within and across dimensions.

Regarding Richard and the required course, there was dissonance within all three dimensions of my ethical framework. Regarding the professional dimension, Richard was not accorded reasonable accommodations, nor was he allowed to make a choice to direct the course and content of his own learning. He was not treated with respect in terms of how he could choose to use his time and money, both of which are important.

Regarding the personal dimension in Richard's case, I chose not to engage with faculty about that particular course at that particular time; thus, I did not have the courage of my convictions, nor was I true to my deepest self.

Situational ethics requires that I follow college policies and procedures and use my authority not for personal gain but in a manner that serves students and promotes the mission of the college. I followed procedures with Richard, but I question whether I served him or ultimately the mission of the college.

If there is dissonance within all three dimensions, identifying dissonance across the dimensions becomes moot. Since all three dimensions were internally dissonant, it might be said that Richard's scenario illustrates negative congruence.

The Impact of Dissonance on the Decision-Maker

In an ideal world, decisions made by a chief academic officer would be congruent within and across professional, personal, and situational ethical dimensions, and such decisions would be viewed by others as ethical and would be supported by them. In reality, a chief academic officer makes decisions every day that fail to meet this ideal. Some decisions generate dissonance within or across dimensions, causing varying degrees of distress to the decision-maker or others. Other decisions may be seen as congruent by the decision-maker, while being viewed as unethical or wrong by others.

Given that ethical issues and their related decisions are of the utmost importance, the very real issue becomes how an administrator retains a sense of integrity, authenticity, and wholeness when he or she experiences dissonance on what may be a daily basis. Almost 50 years ago, psychologist Leon Festinger (1957) identified the phenomenon of cognitive dissonance, which is based on three assumptions: People are sensitive to inconsistencies between their thoughts and their actions; recognition of this inconsistency causes dissonance and motivates the individual to try to resolve the dissonance; and dissonance is resolved in one of three ways—the individual changes his or her beliefs, changes his or her actions, or changes his or her perception of events.

Festinger's framework provides a lens through which areas of dissonance identified in this chapter can be viewed. The possibility exists that changes could occur in beliefs, values, actions, or perceptions, both on the part of the chief academic officer and on the part of other interested parties, which might have the effect of reducing dissonance. However, deeply held beliefs, values, and perceptions may be difficult to change, and actions may already have been taken. Rigorous honesty sometimes precludes making the changes that would result in a neat resolution of complex issues, and doubts may linger. All too often, given the multiplicity of viewpoints, there are no easy answers to questions like the following: What should I have done? What would I do differently? What and to whom is the true commitment?

Ultimately, the chief academic officer must accept that a certain level of dissonance may be unavoidable. He or she must act within a clearly articulated ethical framework and then be willing and able to live with the distress caused by unavoidable dissonance. A CAO needs courage to tolerate dissonance and to remain both centered and responsive while navigating the sometimes treacherous waters of ethical decision-making.

The Role of Courage in Ethical Decision-Making _____

The topic of courage, like the topic of ethics, has been discussed for thousands of years. Current debate concerns the nature of courage and how it is manifested, the source of courage, and whether or not courage can be learned—questions that Plato contemplated 2,400 years ago. Plato's *Laches*, written in approximately 420 B.C.E., is a conversation that occurs among two generals, two elderly Athenians, and Socrates, Plato's teacher. The dialogue centers on the nature of courage (or bravery), whether it can be taught, and if so, whether it is correct to say that courage is a form of knowledge. The dialogue offers several definitions of courage, including the following: To be brave is to stand and fight (behavior); bravery is endurance (a character trait); bravery is knowledge that involves the ability to assess risks accurately (cognitive knowledge); and bravery is the knowledge of good and evil and what is worth fighting for (moral knowledge). The dialogue is inconclusive; it suggests that courage has a range of meanings, and readers are invited to join the discussion and find answers for themselves.

Twenty-four hundred years after it was written, psychologist Sol Rachman (1984, 1990) addressed the questions asked in *Laches* and tried to answer them using empirical research methods. His studies focused on phobias in individuals in extreme situations of war, but his findings have clear implications for a range of educational situations. Rachman identified pathways to fear (i.e., conditioning, vicarious acquisition, and transmission of fear-inducing information) and components of fear (i.e., behavior, subjective discomfort, and physiological response), and he concluded that, in part, courage developed as a result of decoupling these pathways and components. He identified additional factors related to courage, such as self-confidence, skills, motivation, role models, physical and psychological health, and optimism, concepts that imply that courage is a state open to a variety of influences. Rachman defined courage as perseverance or persistence in the face of threat, despite one's fear.

Theologian Paul Tillich (1952) wrote that courage is "the self-affirmation of one's being; so that the most essential part of our being prevails against the less essential" (p. 5). Tillich believed that the courage to *be* affirms the essential self as it participates within the larger context in which life itself is affirmed. He wrote that an individual act of courage was moral if it served a larger, ultimately moral purpose.

Robert Terry (1993), organizational consultant and scholar, discussed authentic leadership as courage in action. He believes that authenticity is necessary for effective and ethical leadership. Fear cuts us off from our authentic self; thus, fear precludes authenticity. Conversely, courage enables or compels us to confront fear, whether fear of the new and unexpected, fear of isolation and separation, fear of difficulty, or fear of lack of direction. Courage allows us to face our fear, ground our thinking and action in authenticity, and build the foundation needed for effective and ethical leadership. According to Terry, "Fear extinguishes leadership and courage ignites leadership" (p. 237).

This brief review of courage gives us the following definitions: Courage is behavior or action (e.g., stand and fight); courage is a character trait (e.g., endurance); courage is based on cognitive knowledge that tells us what to do and how to do it; courage is moral knowledge that tell us what we should do; courage is perseverance in the face of threat, despite one's fear; courage is the self-affirmation of one's being, so that the most essential part of our being prevails against the less essential; and courage is the foundation of authentic, effective, and ethical leadership.

A review of the scenarios in this chapter shows that different types of courage were needed, were present, or were lacking at various times during each scenario. In Anna's situation, it seems courage was not required, because the dimensions of professional, personal, and situational ethics were congruent within and across dimensions. With the math review, it could be said that courage was needed because I stood up for both faculty and students who wanted changes, did what I thought I should do, persevered in the face of threat, and endured the anger of the math faculty because I strongly felt that the interests of both the students and the college were being served. With Richard, I do not believe I displayed any of the types of courage identified.

Earlier in this chapter, I wrote that adherence to moral and ethical principles results in a sense of personal integrity—a state of being whole, entire, and undiminished. If, over time, unavoidable dissonance precludes this feeling of wholeness, one lives a divided life in which one's sense of self and one's sense of personal ethics and integrity exist in a state of controlled fragmentation. Being able to live and function effectively with this fragmentation while continuing to strive for the resolution of fundamental contradictions is a challenge that requires all the different types of courage mentioned here. Perhaps it most particularly requires Tillich's courage to be, in which one strives to discern and then to act in concert with the most essential part of one's being. The challenge of being able to discern the most and least essential factors when all appear to be fundamental is a paradox that cuts to the heart of the courage to be, as Tillich defined it.

Implications for Training and Professional Development

What are the implications of the interface between courage and ethics for professional preparation and training? Effective and ethical administrators must be able to articulate a working philosophy of ethics. An exploration of the nature of courage and its relationship to ethical decision-making and effective leadership would be useful. Finally, chief academic officers in training must understand the challenge involved in retaining a sense of personal integrity and wholeness in situations of unavoidable dissonance. Presenting prospective administrators with scenarios such as those described here may help them situate their own ethical frameworks in real-life contexts and give them opportunities to penetrate the complexity of ethical decision-making.

References_____

Festinger, L. (1957). *A theory of cognitive dissonance.* Evanston, IL: Row & Peterson.

Plato. (1987). Laches. In *Early Socratic dialogues* (I. Lane, Trans.). London, UK: Penguin.

Rachman, S. (1984). Fear and courage. *Behavior Therapy, 15,* 109–120.

Rachman, S. (1990). *Fear and courage* (2nd ed.). New York, NY: Freeman.

Rogers, C. (1978). The formative directional tendency. *Journal of Humanistic Psychology, 18,* 23–26.

Terry, R. W. (1993). *Authentic leadership: Courage in action.* San Francisco, CA: Jossey-Bass.

Tillich, P. (1952). *The courage to be.* New Haven, CT: Yale University Press.

9

Threats to Ethical Leadership: The Hubris of Absolutism, the Politics of Affinity-Based Decision-Making, and the Development of Unethical Followers

David E. Hardy

Regardless of the specific positional role of today's community college leader—president, trustee, administrator, or faculty member—there are continual challenges to acting in an ethical manner while attempting to be effective in what may be one of the most challenging higher education environments in history. For centuries, ethicists have argued the relative merits of what is good for the many versus what is fair to the individual. While such theoretical debates are intellectually stimulating, most community college leaders do not have the luxury of resolving the ethical dilemmas they typically face by simply determining a static personal ethical position and sticking to it. In fact, there may be danger in doing so.

Within community colleges, we expect our leaders to be as strong as a super hero, as wise as King Solomon, as compassionate as Mother Teresa, as financially adept as Donald Trump, as all-seeing as the denizens of Mount Olympus, and, at the end of the day, we also seem to expect them to send each of us home with a lifetime supply of chocolate and other wonderful parting gifts. In short, our organizations and the students and communities they serve demand perfection from our leaders and always stand ready to point out just how one of these leaders has shortchanged one of us or violated our expectations of ethical, moral, or professional behavior. Are we being fair? Perhaps not.

In this chapter, through a series of constructed case studies based on my personal experiences in a variety of leadership roles and that of colleagues from many different community colleges, I discuss the dangers inherent in absolutist ethical posturing, the impact of affinity-based decision-making, and the ways in which leaders sometimes may foster unethical behavior among their followers. I also discuss the limited assistance provided by professional codes of ethics and institutional policies for solving ethical dilemmas and suggest ways in which I have endeavored to calm the cognitive dissonance created by various ethics-challenging situations that I have faced in my own career.

Brady (1990) discusses the importance of considering three different kinds of "rightness" regarding business and professional ethics. First, he indicates that *right doing,* as investigated through the behavioral sciences and theories of moral development, must come into play. Second, he expresses the belief that we must attend to *right being,* or, in other terms, issues of virtue. Lastly, Brady states that we must consider *right knowing,* that is, understanding and utilizing ethical theories of the type discussed in the first part of this volume in dealing with the ethical problems we face in our daily work. Bringing all three of these into play simultaneously requires purposeful effort, so, as we consider what is to follow, I encourage using the mantra "Right Doing, Right Being, Right Knowing" as a touchstone.

I invite the reader now to review and consider a number of situations that *might* confront a community college leader over the course of a month, a week, or, in some cases, a day or two. I suggest, too, that the reader attempt to make a decision about what she or he would do in each situation as he or she moves through the scenario. In the cases in which a series of actions is taken, the reader might also take note of the decisions the leader in the story makes and how those decisions comport with the reader's personal code of ethics. The goal of this exercise is to encourage each reader to formulate his or her own solutions to the problems, rather than have the text supply them.

Each constructed case presented here shares features with situations that I have personally experienced or with stories that community college leaders from across the country have shared with me over many years.

None of them exactly duplicates a real situation, however, so they must be regarded as fictional.

The Hubris of Absolutism

I'll introduce the first two cases by saying a word about my professional experience. Throughout my administrative career, people often have called me "The Policy Guy." My colleagues, employees, and supervisors have typically looked to me when a "rules issue" has arisen, because they know that if there is a rule, I tend to know what it is and where to find it in the many policy manuals that govern the day-to-day operations of an institution. I also have been considered relatively unbending in terms of conforming to those policies. As a rule, my professional position has been that if someone has created a written policy, there must be a very good reason for it, and therefore every employee has a sworn duty to uphold the policy.

For much of my career, I also have made many attempts to create and internalize my own unwritten "personal policy manual" in terms of professional ethics and criteria for decision-making. Unfortunately, this has proven in the main to be an ulcer-producing challenge and, on occasion, has led to administrative nightmares for me and for others.

I am guessing I am not the only one who has made hard and fast rules for myself, only to be confronted with situations in which, with every fiber of my being, I know that compliance with my own rule is not the right thing to do. By way of exploring this particular ethical conundrum, I offer two cases loosely based on situations I have encountered in recent years.

The Special Student

Marie is the first person in her family ever to attend a college or university. She works 40 hours a week, cares for two children as a single mother, and is enrolled in four courses this semester. She also serves as a Student Ambassador and as the vice president of the honor society. Furthermore, she is a favorite student of the college president's, a true role model for other young first-generation students and single mothers, and a popular student leader.

This semester, Marie's children have been sick, causing her to be absent four times from one of her courses. The instructor's policy is that five absences cause a student's final grade to be dropped one full letter. Marie has been selected for an academic award that carries with it a $5,000 scholarship and recognition in the statewide and national press. To receive the scholarship, however, Marie must attend an out-of-state ceremony and banquet that falls on the same day as the course in which she has the four absences. She has asked the instructor for an exception to his rule, but he has refused, saying it is not his problem that the awards ceremony is scheduled on his class day, and that Marie will simply have to make a choice. She knows, too, that having her grade dropped one letter in this course will negatively affect her overall GPA and make her a much less competitive candidate for another large scholarship she is pursuing to enable her to transfer to a four-year university after she graduates this spring.

You are the dean of students. Marie has come to you, told you of her predicament, and asked you to intervene on her behalf with the faculty member. By policy and practice, administrators do not interfere in the grading policies of faculty members; furthermore, as dean, you have a firm personal stand against advocating for students to try to persuade faculty members to make exceptions to their class rules, and you have never done so before. What do you do?

The Dying Program

As the vice president of academic affairs at your small, rural community college, you have responsibility for analyzing the fiscal viability of all academic and technical education programs housed on your campus. You must also review all programs annually to determine which, if any, need to be closed due to continuing low enrollments, low degree production, and overly burdensome costs of operation. With the endorsement of the college's board of trustees and president, you have put into place an annual program review model and policy that utilizes purely quantitative measures and comparative analyses of all programs under your purview.

Over the past few years, you have had to close a number of programs with fairly short histories. This year, the president is pressing you to close a particularly expensive program in industrial technology that has for the past five years steadily declined in enrollment, completions, and dollars produced through tuition and state funding support. This program has been offered at your college for 23 years under the leadership of the same instructor. This instructor has two years before he can retire from the college with a full pension and, unfortunately, seems to have no transferable skills or credentials that would make reassignment to another technical education program viable.

You have always made your decisions about program closure by the numbers, but this faculty member is well liked by students, peers, and other staff members and administrators and is also a leader in the faculty senate. Do you follow your standard practice and close the program without regard to the effect on this loyal employee, or do you operate outside of your own policy and attempt to advocate for some alternative solution with your president who clearly wants the program closed this year?

■ *Discussion*

In each of the preceding cases, the conflict is one between what the leader has accepted as a set of hard and fast rules concerning decision-making within her or his administrative role at the institution, and the particulars of what she or he sees as a unique or special situation. I have met many administrators who, in an effort to smooth their decision-making pathway, have attempted to put in place an internal set of ethical absolutes, or have attempted to rely on the bureaucratic ethics policy embedded in their operations manual, trying never to vary from the use of these tools. I know some who claim that they always rely on a "utilitarian model," an "ethics of caring," or some other general moral/ethical model that is taught in some philosophy class or religious tradition. Likewise, I have encountered those who, not unlike myself, have attempted to rely on whatever the board, the institutional leadership, the state, or the profession has "passed into law" in arbitrating every either/or decision in an effort to depersonalize responsibility for the decision made.

As can be seen in these two cases, taking an absolute stand based on precedent or the "rule of law" (such as it may be) will mean that someone or something will lose. If we take the position of attempting to create the greatest good for the greatest number, do we not have to disregard the needs of the individual student or faculty member who will be negatively affected? In contrast, if we take care of the two individuals in the cases using a belief that we should do no harm to the least among us, might we not be negatively affecting the other students in the class who are still expected to comply with the faculty member's rules since they are not "stars," or might we take resources away from those faculty members and students involved in the programs at the institution that are meeting the requirements for program continuation that are outlined in the program review policy?

As with so many decisions the administrator has to make, these have very real power to create good or ill in the lives of real people. How do we find balance on a case-by-case basis and, more importantly, how do we judge each case when we know that others see—rightly or wrongly—each decision as setting a precedent that will affect future situations and outcomes? Lastly, how do we avoid being so prideful about our reliance on a static, structured decision-making model that we are not trapped by it as we navigate the many decisions that we make within an institution over the years of our careers? These issues, I believe, are at the heart of this problem that I have called "the hubris of absolutism."

The Politics of Affinity-Based Decision-Making _____

Using the same constructed case study approach, I turn now to a different kind of threat to our personal and professional ethics that we often face as community college leaders. The next set of cases, representative of situations that are all too common in today's politicized community college environment, investigates the challenge of making choices that require faculty members, administrators, and trustees to look beyond their personal preferences and characteristics—their affinities—in order to provide the kind of leadership that is deemed ethical and fair by those whom they lead and serve.

My own background is in the performing arts. As such, I have a natural affinity for instructional programs and community outreach efforts in theater, film, dance, and music, as well as an appreciation for the visual arts and a firm belief in the importance of all these disciplines within the academy. As a result, wherever I have been employed I have quickly sought out "those arts people" and looked for ways to support and participate in their work, even if there is nothing in my job description that would require me to do so.

Conversely, I have never considered myself (after that overly challenging advanced placement chemistry course in high school) to have much in common with those folks who study and teach the natural sciences. It was never that I could not do the work that they do; I just did not care for it much. Therefore, I often have thought of the faculty, students, and administrators in these disciplines as "the other." On occasion, I have purposely avoided them, but more often, I have simply acknowledged their presence and then devoted my time to those things that have interested me more. Call it a sin of omission, if you will.

As I reflect on my work as an academic leader, three different tasks—the mentoring of new faculty, the development of operational budgets, and the review of program viability—have proven particularly challenging in this regard. I invite the reader to consider the following cases based on these three aspects of academic leadership.

Mentoring New Faculty: Doting Dad or Forgetful Father?

Academic leaders at the department chair level and above (e.g., deans and vice presidents) typically have responsibility for the mentoring of new faculty. As an academic dean, in one year, you have 15 first-year and second-year faculty members, in nearly as many disciplines, to whom you have some responsibility for mentoring and acclimating to your institution. Some are in the performing and fine arts, some are in the natural and social sciences, and others are in education, mathematics, English, foreign language, and speech communications.

Your own background is in the natural sciences, and you also have an affinity for mathematics. You are not very interested in the performing and visual arts, the social sciences, language arts, or education fields of study. You find ways to connect with the new faculty in science and math much more readily than with those who are outside your areas of interest and expertise. However, you cannot ignore the needs of the other new faculty members; this would not be right. You often find yourself feeling like a proud and doting father toward the scientists and mathematicians, wanting them to be very successful and working with them to accomplish their goals. Conversely, while you find the other new faculty members interesting, engaged, and true assets to your institution, you sometimes feel like an absentee father who, while he loves his children, often helps them only when they seek him out for specific support.

As a leader of multiple academic disciplines, are you ethically obligated to treat all these valuable new employees in the same way? If so, how might you do a better job of being equitable in terms of making sure everyone's needs are being met?

Budget Development: Philanthropist or Skinflint?

You are the vice president of business affairs at an inner-city community college that serves a very diverse student population, a position to which you rose two years ago after serving as the director of information technology at the institution for five years. Before that, you taught as a member of the computer science faculty for over a decade. Your institution has both a Title V institutional improvement grant, because of its status as a Hispanic-Serving Institution (HSI), and a National Science Foundation (NSF) grant.

The Title V grant is being used to improve student performance in developmental reading and writing. The NSF grant project is aimed at bringing more students into computer science and mathematics. Both grants fund specialized tutoring for the disciplines on which they focus, and the funding for both grants is ending this fiscal year. In your analysis of funds availability for the coming year, you find that the college only has sufficient dollars of its own to support the continuation of specialized tutoring services in one of these two areas.

You know that the college president will accept your recommendation concerning which tutoring program to continue. Given your natural affinity for and interest in computer science, how do you ensure that you make the right recommendation and, as important, that your decision is not interpreted by faculty and administrators at the college as based on your own connection to the computer science program and profession?

Program Review: The Microscope Versus the Telescope

As discussed in an earlier case, institutions often conduct periodic reviews of instructional programs to determine whether they continue to be fiscally viable and to meet the needs of the students and communities that the institution serves. You are the president of a suburban community college located in a predominantly white, middle-class community in the South. You moved into this position six years ago after serving as an academic vice president at another community college within your statewide system, and before that, you were a member of the music faculty at that same college. You have a particular interest in ethnomusicology, specifically in the African-American musical heritage of the southeastern United States.

You have just received the program review data from your institutional research officer and see that, for the fifth year in a row, there are two programs at your college that appear to be serving small numbers of students while consuming large amounts of operating capital: the music program and the only diagnostic medical sonography program within a 100-mile radius. In the past, you have been criticized for closing down low-performing allied health programs while allowing performing arts programs, which are typically "loss leaders" at community colleges, to continue. Faculty in the allied health and technical programs believe you are not fair and equitable in your treatment of their programs and that, because you are a musician by training, you let faculty members in the arts continue to spend the institution's money on things that interest you, but do not appear to interest the college's surrounding community.

What do you do this year, and how do you ethically justify your decision? Are there other considerations beyond the story in the quantitative data that you should take into account? Can you just let the evidence speak for itself, use the data, and close both programs? Alternatively, can you close one and not the other and still feel that you have acted in a responsible and ethical manner?

▥ *Discussion*

While I base my examples on an affinity for the pursuit of knowledge and skills in a particular set of academic disciplines, many other examples abound within our field. I have witnessed decision-making based on each and every personal factor that is not supposed to be considered when making decisions about people (i.e., gender, race, ethnicity, sexual orientation, age, socioeconomic status, and disability status) or about policies, programs, and practices (e.g., the popularity or lack thereof of a program or its staff within the institution or the community; the relationship of the program to the decision-makers; the personal or professional effect of a decision on the decision-maker; and resistance to the implementation of a new policy or practice by institutional actors).

Is any one of these types of affinity-based decision-making more legitimate than another? Must the administrator be "true to the group" that she or he represents, or to which he or she belongs, at the price of being unfair to members of groups with which the administrator has no affinity, or is doing so a personal choice which, in turn, carries personal responsibility?

The Development of Unethical Followers_____

The third and perhaps most challenging set of cases explores the role of the leader in developing ethical followers within the organization. The popular press is replete with stories of subordinates in business, government, and education whose unethical actions have placed their leaders and their organizations at great risk. Typically, these operatives are acting the way they believe their leaders expect them to act, though this is not always the case. Community college leaders have the difficult task of ensuring that those who work in their institutions are not creating situations that are ethically unsound.

My father has always been fond of saying, "Everybody has a boss, Son." By this, he means that because, in our professional lives, each of us reports to someone who theoretically has some amount of say-so over our actions at work, there is always at least one other party who either tells us what to do or lets us do everything that we do for a paycheck. My father's comment usually came quickly on the heels of some account I would give him of some action I had witnessed in my work that I had found absolutely unbelievable in terms of its ethics or morality. His response would indicate that, in his mind, no one gets away with anything that the person to whom she or he reports does not explicitly or implicitly sanction. As stated earlier, however, I doubt this is always the case.

In my own community college experience, I have found that there are at least four different types of scenarios that can involve wrong action by an institution's employees or students. In the first scenario, the supervisor specifically directs the employee to take an action that he knows is not ethical. In the second, the supervisor creates a goal for the employee and leaves the employee to work out his or her own way of getting the job done. In the third, the supervisor implies his desire for a particular outcome but does not direct any specific employee to take a specific action. In the last scenario, the supervisor has no knowledge of what the employee is doing or why he or she is doing it. To illustrate, let us look at each of these situations using a brief case.

The Evil Emperor

The community college president wants a "clean bill of health" in the upcoming evaluation by the regional accrediting agency. He tells his chief academic officer simply to remove all of the documents related to improperly credentialed faculty members from the files and to leave the names of these faculty members off the roster presented to the visiting committee. The chief academic officer complies with the request.

The Imprecise Sovereign

The dean in charge of social sciences is concerned with the high drop rates in social science courses and tells the faculty members who teach in those disciplines that the problem must be fixed immediately, but he does not tell them how to do this. The anthropology faculty get together and decide that the best way to reduce the drop rate is to tell students in their courses that they will all receive grades of A as long as they stay in the class until the end of the semester, regardless of how they perform on examinations and whether they actually submit the research paper that the syllabus indicates is required.

The Manipulating Monarch

During a staff meeting, the chief student affairs officer remarks that she wishes the number of admissions applications received by the community college would increase during the current academic year, since she is evaluated in part on this particular measurement. Hearing this, a student recruiter formulates a plan to visit a number of area locations where individuals can be convinced to complete the admissions application even though they have no intention of actually enrolling at the college. The recruiter knows that this will make him look good to the student affairs officer and that actually getting the students to enroll—that is, "closing the sale"—is someone else's responsibility.

The Oblivious Overlord

An employee in the business office in charge of auxiliary services at the community college consistently manipulates the wording in requests for proposals so that only one vendor can actually meet the bid requirements. This vendor regularly provides the college with a large donation to its scholarship fund, and the employee knows that this donation would no longer occur if the vendor did not keep winning contracts. She also knows that the specific bidding requirements really are not necessary and that, if they were not included, a number of area vendors would easily be able to provide lower bids for the desired goods and services. Neither the vice president of financial affairs nor any other supervisor with oversight of this employee's daily work has ever indicated to the employee that the scholarship money is more important to the college than a fair bidding process, but she personally feels this is the case.

▣ *Discussion*

In each of these four scenarios, the employee has done something that many would consider unethical. The ethics of the leader most certainly could also be called into question in the first three cases. Could not the same be true in the last case? Is ignorance of an employee's actions a defense for a leader or supervisor?

In his discussions of servant leadership, Greenleaf (1977) speaks extensively of the important role that the development of "good followership" has in the creation and maintenance of great leadership. These scenarios all could be seen as a breakdown of that process and possibly as illustrations of poor leadership just as easily as they could be viewed as illustrations of unethical behavior by institutional actors in non-leadership roles. As you reflect on these cases, what responsibility do you ascribe to the leaders in each and, more importantly, what could be done to improve the way that these administrators are socializing those employees that report to them?

Is There Any Guidance That Can Really Help?_____

Earlier in this chapter, I mentioned my reputation as an arbiter of policy and a knowledge base of institutional rules and regulations at the various institutions where I have worked. What guidance, however, do formal documents related to ethical behavior give us regarding the kinds of ethical dilemmas that I have outlined herein? Oftentimes, the assistance they provide is scant or off target and, on occasion, it is nonexistent.

Primarily, formal guidelines of two types are available relating to ethics for professionals employed at institutions of higher education. The first are the codes of professional ethics created and endorsed by the various professional associations and organizations. These are not dissimilar from those that exist for doctors, lawyers, and other professionals, and they present a set of ethical standards to which members of the profession (or at least of the association) should adhere. The second kind of formal guidelines are those that appear as standards of conduct within the policy documents of the institutions of higher education themselves.

Faculty members have a code of ethics of the first variety outlined by the American Association of University Professors and other instructional organizations (AAUP, 1987). Institutional researchers also have a code of ethics endorsed by their professional organization, the Association for Institutional Research (AIR, 2001). Likewise, student affairs professionals have a code of ethics set forth by the American College Personnel Association (ACPA, 2006), and an ethical code is provided for financial aid administrators by their association, the National Association of Student Financial Aid Administrators (NASFAA, 1999). Similar codes of professional ethics exist for many other individual administrative groups (e.g., business officers and planners) within community colleges and universities.

Perhaps more importantly, the American Association of University Administrators developed a document in 2004 titled *Professional Standards of the AAUA*. While the membership of this organization is primarily made up of administrators at four-year institutions, the AAUA's mission statement does indicate that it represents higher education administrators at all types of colleges and universities. The AAUA's document, through a rather interesting set of pairings of administrators' rights and responsibilities, offers what may be considered an overly succinct, sometimes glib, outline of what is moral and ethical in terms of nondiscrimination, use of resources, professional development, job evaluation procedures, development of job descriptions, authority and support, career advancement, policy development, speaking for the institution and making statements of personal opinion, academic freedom (of the administrator and others), personal privacy, and other issues (AAUA, 2004). Weingartner (1999) points out, however, that this document appears to be more concerned with the welfare of college and university administrators than with the welfare of and obligation to the "clients" that these administrators are meant to serve.

Lastly, and most relevant to this discussion, in 2005 the American Association of Community Colleges (AACC) formulated a recommended code of ethics for community college chief executive officers. This document addresses the CEO's ethical responsibilities to members of the board; to other administrators, faculty, and staff employed at the institution; to students; to other educational institutions; and to businesses, civic groups, and the community at large. It is filled with the currently popular rhetoric of excellence, quality, open communication and open access, equity, and

Like the other statements of ethical principles, however, it
.o define ethics and ethical action beyond what is intuitive, and
, no guidance on how the CEO should go about ensuring her or his
.ons are always ethical, or how to choose among difficult options, each
of which might violate one part of the ethical code in the course of com-
plying with another.

The AACC document contains four basic tenets for ethical action that
CEOs should consider: trust and respect for all individuals; honesty in all
actions; just and fair treatment of all people; and integrity in all actions.
Similarly imprecise rhetoric appears in the ethical codes and statements of
principle of all of the other organizations referenced here. I question the
value of such language, however. What community college administrator—or any other human being, for that matter—would flatly state that he
or she did not think it was important and a matter of common practice always to act justly, fairly, honestly, and with integrity, or that he or she did
not always strive to show trust and respect to all people, even if docu-
mented actions might provide evidence to the contrary? I would say, generally, that only a fool would do so, and, certainly, no one who wanted to
maintain a high-ranking position in a public institution would be so
brazen as to claim that any one of these ideals is not important or desirable.
So, in practice, what good does the adoption of this rhetoric actually do for
our institutions and our leaders?

The difficulty with profession-specific ethics statements, as I have discussed previously (Hardy, 2002), is that they often do not address some of
the specific situations in which community colleges leaders often find
themselves. Rather, they tend to be gloriously couched statements of what
the "perfect being" within the field would be like. If we choose to base our
own ethical standards on these documents, we can find answers to some
problems, but not to all of them. If guidance exists at all, it appears more
clearly in those statements that address narrowly drawn professional
groups like the institutional researchers or the student affairs professionals,
whose job-related duties, at least to some degree, dictate what they will be
doing on a day-to-day basis and thus include more situation-specific direc-
tives. The assistance provided by statements aimed at more broadly drawn
constituencies—all university administrators, all faculty members, or all
chief executive officers—without regard to the environment in which they
operate, the stakeholders they serve, or the work they actually do, is much
less substantial.

In another vein, institutions typically have at least some guidance of an ethical nature embedded into their policy manuals. As noted in prior work (Hardy, 2002), most colleges and universities have such ethics statements within these board-approved documents, but what is included is generally there to protect the institution (and the board) from litigation and to show compliance with outside regulation and statutory law. These guidelines limit the actions of employees surrounding such issues as the acceptance of gifts, nepotism, conflicts of interest, alcohol and drug use, sexual harassment and discrimination, whistle-blowing, perjury and falsification, fraud and embezzlement, and other offenses that could be litigated. In general, these documents tend to be of the "thou shalt not" variety and, like the professional codes of ethics, do not do a good job of either defining ethical action—except by pointing out what it is not—or of providing guidance to administrators by creating an ethical model of decision-making for the institution and its employees. While the professional codes focus on individual perfection, these documents tend to inform employees about how to avoid breaking the law or getting the institution sued, rather than assisting them in addressing the ethical dilemmas for which no statute or regulation exists—the very kind of dilemmas I have illustrated here and that confront us as academic leaders every day.

Still, each type of guideline does have some value and is, if nothing else, a necessary tool in today's litigious world. The wise community college leader will, at the very least, be knowledgeable about all such guidelines that affect his or her daily work life. Likewise, the wise community college leader brings together employees working under each of the different professional codes for crucial conversations about the ways in which these various ethical codes and guidelines may appear to be in conflict. Institutions and their leaders can only be well served through such discussion, for only by revealing and investigating such "between-codes" conflicts can these conflicts can be resolved and institutional policies and practices become better aligned.

So, What Is the Bottom Line?

I hope that, as the reader has pondered the situations in each of the cases presented here, it has become clear that "right knowing, right doing, and right being" are a constant challenge to the community college administrator, faculty member, or staff employee. How do we know what to do, when to do it, and how? Are there any standardized guidelines that make this all easier by giving us one set of concrete rules on which to base every decision that we make? Conversely, might not Fletcher's (1964) model of situational ethics be the one of the few that makes sense for a community college leader to use, if he or she simply must have a formal theoretical framework to serve as a foundation for his or her work?

Fletcher (1964) posited the belief that all decision-making should be based not on fixed law but, rather, on the circumstances of a particular situation. For Fletcher, love (specifically, *agapē,* a non-sexual form of love that is volitional, unconditional, and nondiscriminating) is the only absolute and should be the sole motive underlying every decision that we make. Additionally, in Fletcher's model, justice is the distribution of this type of love for others rather than slavish compliance with the letter of the law. Further, this model is based on the belief that the ethical nature (or morality) of any given act is a function of the state of the system in which it occurs at specific time that the act is performed.

Since Fletcher's original development of his model, situational ethics has been interpreted—by both opponents and proponents of the model—as having other meanings and implications beyond these; however, I would suggest that the original, simple tenets of this ethical belief system might be important to consider. If we recast the multiple professional codes of ethics that I have referenced here and look at the fundamental beliefs that they incorporate, do they not tell us, essentially, to do the right things for others, regardless of who the others are, while bearing in mind all of the particulars of a given situation and avoiding, as much as possible, harm to others beyond those involved most directly in our decision? This, it would seem to me, is fully in keeping with Fletcher's original ideals.

After all, at the end of the day, are not all of these cases really about objectivity? Is it not often the case that our own myopia causes many of our ethical dilemmas in discharging our administrative and leadership duties within our institutions? I believe most of us do our level best to be objective in our daily decision-making within the institutions that we lead. Nonetheless, we sometimes stand too close to a problem to see it for what it really may be and, sadly, view it from either a single perspective or only a limited number of perspectives. In the past, to avoid this barrier to good, ethical decision-making, I always found it useful to do two different kinds of examination.

First, within the formal organizations or institutions in which I have worked, I have always been a proponent of collaborative decision-making and shared responsibility. I have found that the avoidance of totalitarian rule—my own or others—has always gone far in protecting my institution and me from making foolish decisions that appear to be unethical. Well-constructed, representative groups of faculty, administrators, staff members, and students can often provide a system of checks and balances for us as individual administrators, and I strongly encourage leaders to create one for themselves, even if it is informal.

I do know, too, of a number of community colleges that have actually created institutional committees on ethics—not unlike the ethical oversight committees that exist within many companies and organizations outside of higher education—that provide a "moral rudder" for their institutions. While we are often all too quick to "form a committee" at our colleges to deal with every little thing, a committee of this sort might be an important one to have, especially if the institution is in the midst of trying times or if numerous ethical challenges are being raised both inside and outside the walls. Might it not better to be a partner with those whom you lead in finding ethical solutions that represent the institution's collective conscience, than to attempt to create the appearance that we alone are a bastion of fairness and justice? I think that it would.

Second, I think it is wise to take counsel from outside of the institution. I have a wonderful former colleague who has often said to me, upon seeing someone walking down the street in clothing that he or she just should not be wearing out in public, "They really need a best friend. If they had one, they would tell them that outfit was made for someone else to wear, and that they need to go home and change." I think that, in the most practical sense, community college administrators need this sort of "best friend," too, professionally speaking.

I am firmly convinced that having a "best friend" of this sort with whom we can have frank, honest, open conversations about the ethical dilemmas that we face on a daily basis can do wonders for community college leaders. While the development of ethical models and, in fact, of all philosophies tends to be presented to us in our philosophy and ethics courses and readings as a very solitary endeavor, the movement from theory to practice in a world filled with other actors will, I believe, always derive great benefit from conversation with at least one other person that we believe, to borrow from the AACC's (2005) rhetoric, to be trustworthy and respectful of all persons, honest, just, fair, and brimming with integrity. All too often, we attempt to solve the kinds of ethical paradoxes I have illustrated here only through the best efforts of the debating society that exists in each of our minds. I encourage leaders, instead, to invite at least one other person into that conversation, since, sadly, it sometimes is our own best thinking that may have caused the conundrum to occur in the first place. Personally, I have found that this, above all other tools of the trade, has enabled me to make what I believe to have been the best-judged ethical decisions in my career and, as a result, to sleep well at the end of the day.

So, when we must decide what to do about a long-term employee in a failing program, an excellent student who wants exceptional treatment, the child of a friend who wants a job, or how to distribute the college's ever-shrinking financial resources, I invite us to do three things. First, ask ourselves three questions: Would I do what I am about to do if the situation involved a different person or group of people? Is there anyone who may be harmed by the course of action that I am about to take? Am I taking into account all of the realities of the situation right here and right now? Then, call a trusted confidant, explain the entire situation, and ask if there is anything we are missing, any holes in our line of reasoning, or if our decision is sound. Finally, if all else fails, do what we are so inclined to do these days in higher education: Get a group of colleagues together to discuss the situation in order to get multiple perspectives. Remember always that the decisions we make individually as leaders often are ascribed to our institutions as "whole beings." Thus, to ensure that the decisions reflect the institution's collective conscience, it is never wrong to bring others into the decision-making process when the stakes are high and people's lives are involved.

References

American Association of Community Colleges. (2005). *Recommended code of ethics for chief executive officers of community colleges.* Retrieved January 26, 2007, from www.aacc.nche.edu/Template.cfm?Section=Position _Statements&Template=/InterestDisplay.cfm&InterestCategoryID=224

American Association of University Administrators. (2004). *Mission and professional standards of the AAUA.* Retrieved December 1, 2006, from www.aaua.org/about/mission.html

American Association of University Professors. (1987). *Statement on professional ethics.* Retrieved December 1, 2006, from www.aaup.org /AAUP/pubsres/policydocs/statementonprofessionalethics.htm

American College Personnel Association. (2006). *Statement of ethical principles and standards.* Washington, DC: Author.

Association for Institutional Research. (2001). *Code of ethics for institutional research.* Washington, DC: Author.

Brady, F. N. (1990). *Ethical managing: Rules and results.* New York, NY: Macmillan.

Fletcher, J. F. (1964). *Situation ethics: The new morality.* Philadelphia, PA: Westminster.

Greenleaf, R. K. (1977). *Servant leadership: A journey into the nature of legitimate power and greatness.* Ramsey, NJ: Paulist Press.

Hardy, D. E. (2002, June). Ethical considerations affecting teaching in community colleges: An abundance of feelings and limited facts. *Community College Journal of Research and Practice, 26*(5), 383–399.

National Association of Student Financial Aid Administrators. (1999). *Statement of ethical principles.* Retrieved December 1, 2006, from www.nasfaa.org/annualpubs/NEthical599.html

Weingartner, R. H. (1999). *The moral dimensions of academic administration.* Lanham, MD: Rowman & Littlefield.

10

Leading From the Head and the Heart

Susan K. Chappell

An amazing fact of life is that sometimes, even when an answer seems so intuitively obvious, it isn't. A corollary to this fact of life is that sometimes when dilemmas seem most murky and shrouded in peripheral and seemingly irrelevant conditions, in truth, there is but one real and proper way to proceed. This chapter about such situations, but the topic is far from new.

Second Verse, Same as the First (Or Is That the Thirty-Second Verse?)

In an article published in the *Harvard Business Review* in 1989, Kenneth Andrews noted,

> Making ethical decisions is easy when the facts are clear and the choices are black and white. But it is a different story when the situation is clouded by ambiguity, incomplete information, multiple points of view, and conflicting responsibilities. . . . Ethical decisions depend on both the decision-making process itself and on the experience, intelligence, and integrity of the decision-maker. (p. 100)

More recently, Robert Starratt (2005, p. 125) outlined five domains of ethical responsibility for educators, noting that a person must fully carry out the responsibilities at each sequential level before he or she can perform reliably at the next level. These domains are the following:

1. Responsibility as a human being.

2. Responsibility as a citizen and public servant.

3. Responsibility as an educator.

4. Responsibility as an educational administrator.

5. Responsibility as an educational leader.

By mere label, these domains succinctly illustrate the complexity of the burdens faced by today's leaders in not only performing their day-to-day duties, but even more significantly in confronting the multifaceted dilemmas associated with equity, diversity, quality, performance, and the myriad other types of issues they face in their constantly evolving roles.

The Challenges of Leadership

Recognizing the thousands of lives that we as educational leaders impact during the course of our careers, it is important to acknowledge that even our most casual comments and seemingly unimportant actions are subject to a higher standard of scrutiny. This level of scrutiny increases with every advancement we achieve in our careers. Is this an ethical dilemma? No, but certainly our personal sense of ethics is verified or challenged on a larger stage because of this reality. Ethical dilemmas present themselves in even the simplest of circumstances, but the most difficult ones present themselves when there is conflict between what the leader knows or feels to be right and his or her sense that acting in this way might somehow put the welfare of another human being in jeopardy.

When It Comes to Downsizing

Most colleges today are faced with tough program and project decisions surrounding prioritizing, assessing efficiency and cost/benefit, and verifying compatibility with their mission. Many a worthy project is not pursued, not funded, or discontinued after a successful start because it cannot be justified either within the context of the college mission or in light of constrained resources.

Such was the case with Milo. An energetic young staff person at a relatively large community college, Milo was in most observers' eyes a rising star in the organization. He was reliable, punctual, and often on duty far after the workday had ended. Milo was the kind of employee that most supervisors wish they had, in multiples of 10.

Within a couple of years, Milo had not only improved the systems that helped him manage his given responsibilities as coordinator of job placement, but he had also gone the extra mile to provide other assistance to the students he served. No longer was he merely placing students and graduates in career-related positions in the community and monitoring their successes on the job; he often was finding ways to assist with after-school care for their children and was even helping them in their efforts to transfer to neighboring institutions after they had graduated from the college. He was commended for this extra effort, and in time his successes yielded him considerable acclaim.

Then came the disturbing news that a severe funding crisis plaguing the state was ultimately going to affect every public college, including Milo's. The president called for each administrator to seriously assess what was happening within his or her area of responsibility and to make recommendations for cutting whatever activities were not mission critical. Further, the directive came for leaders within the organization to expect that 10%–15% of the college's staff would need to be released before the start of the next fiscal year.

Suddenly, Milo found that his job was in jeopardy. Students and staff alike rallied to support him, but Milo could not show that his work was critically tied to the mission of the institution. His supervisor defended him as a well-qualified and hardworking employee, but could not defend the work that had come to consume most of Milo's average day. His position was eliminated, and the support staff, who by this time were managing all the technical details of job placement and follow-up, were left to do the job, with moderate increases in title and compensation.

Discussion Questions

1. Is there someone to "blame" for this unfortunate loss of a valuable human resource?

2. How could such laudable services to students result in the demise of a worthy employee?

3. Were there other options for handling this situation?

▦ *Reflection*

This scenario calls attention to the relationship among job descriptions, evaluations, and institutional mission—a relationship that cannot be dismissed as bureaucratically inconsequential. The old adage about hiring only the best needs a postscript: Hire only the best and then keep these best focused and in tune with long-term and short-term goals of the organization, never losing sight of how they relate to the overall institutional mission and vision. If Milo's excellent work with students and graduates had been part of a project that had been purposefully planned with a desired outcome related to a college goal, this story might have ended differently.

Struggles With References

Professor Randolph was hired mid-year as a temporary faculty member, replacing someone who was forced unexpectedly to leave his post, with no time for a full-fledged search before the start of the next term. In spite of a record of short-term stays with her previous employers, Professor Randolph's interview was excellent, and her teaching demonstration was most impressive. The only regret was that the college could not bring Professor Randolph on board permanently; but such is the way with an integrity-driven search process. Professor Randolph accepted the offer of a temporary appointment with the understanding that she would be eligible to compete for the position once the full search was under way.

As the term progressed, Professor Randolph began to show signs that she was not the ideal professor everyone had perceived her to be. For a number of reasons, she did not win the position when the official search closed in early summer. There was much protest, but the decision stood. Professor Randolph was forced to seek other employment, which by this time was noted as a clear pattern in her work history. While there were concerns on a number of fronts, nothing of particular note had made its way into the personnel files of previous employers.

As coincidence would have it, one of Professor Randolph's prospective new employers had ties to the college where she had completed her temporary faculty assignment. Not surprisingly, a reference call was made and the college leader had to decide what was appropriate to reveal, and what was not.

Discussion Questions

1. How does one balance personal perceptions with duty so as not to jeopardize permanently someone's future when specific evidence or documentation is lacking?

2. Is there a duty to "tell all"?

3. Absent legal responsibility to reveal the negative in such an instance, how should a leader share information when the "right" questions are not asked by the prospective employer?

4. What are the "right" questions?

▥ *Reflection*

Providing references has become an increasingly difficult part of a leader's job, and the hesitation to offer full disclosure has become a normal reaction, in part because of the consequences that have ensued when leaders insert personal opinions or exaggerate the importance of singular situations when trying to offer candid perceptions about an employee's past performance. The rule of thumb has become, "The less said, the better." It is far safer to respond succinctly to the questions than to expound or try to lead the prospective employer down a path the employer has not designed him- or herself. From the opposite perspective, a leader can easily understand the importance of designing questions that create maximum opportunities to elicit insightful and accurate observations.

The often-used final interview question, "Is there anything else you would like to add?" creates too many opportunities for responses that reflect personality-driven attitudes and potentially irrelevant facts. A better approach might be for the leader to reframe such a question: "If given the opportunity, would I rehire this individual?" The answer to that question, even if the response comes in the form of a single word, and the inflection used in giving the answer, speak volumes.

Helping Students . . . Or Not?

Rita, a student, entered the dean's office one evening upset to the point of distress. Her neck and arms flared with red spots—hives, she said, explaining that they occurred whenever she reached such a state of exasperation. She was accompanied by a classmate, who was there more to make sure Rita was okay than to complain himself, although he confirmed that

Rita's accounts of her professor and his actions were accurate and not exaggerated.

Rita's frustration was the result of problematic issues that had been accumulating over the whole semester, including the professor's consistent tardiness to class, his constant adjustments to already vaguely stated rules in the syllabus, and his unwillingness to be flexible with a personal dilemma that had prevented Rita from completing an important final assignment on schedule. How could he, she asked the dean, refuse such flexibility when the entire class had exhibited exceptional tolerance and flexibility toward him for the duration of the term?

Now, Rita's otherwise very good grade was in jeopardy. Rather than arguing the point in class, however, she exited in the midst of the session and made her way downstairs to see the dean. When the dean asked what remedy she was seeking, Rita could not answer. She did not wish for her complaint to be taken forward, as she feared retribution from the professor.

Discussion Questions

1. What is the educational leader's responsibility: to honor anonymity or to pursue an investigation into suspected poor conduct? Is there a difference in the degree of responsibility owed to faculty as compared to students, or vice versa?

2. How much data (versus intuition) are needed or required to launch an investigation? Can an administrator use previous knowledge of similar behavior in such a case?

3. Are there ways to address situations such as Rita's without revealing the source of the allegations?

4. What are the consequences of pursuing a complaint when the professor feels equally violated and not at fault?

▨ Reflection

Administrative leaders are taught the importance of supporting the faculty and other members of their team, thus presenting a united front on the part of the institution. At the same time, however, leaders are also responsible for making sure students know their rights and options for filing objections without fear of punishment. If a student is persistent and determined in filing an objection, this persistence and determination could be indications that there is at least some truth to the allegation of impropriety. It is incumbent on the leader to gather and understand all of the facts and to be able to clearly distinguish these facts from rumors and second-hand information.

Abandoning Protocol in the Name of What Is Right: Jackie's Story

As a member of an organization's team, one must be prepared to act in accordance with the standards and expectations set by the leadership, or be willing to leave the team if personal and organizational values are incompatible. Valuable information on job fit and person-organization fit has been a topic of interest for researchers since at least the early 1970s (Bretz & Judge, 1994; Caplan & Van Harrison, 1993; Stern, 1970). While no wise and aspiring leader would purposely pursue a position that requires him or her to abandon personal honesty and integrity for the sake of loyalty to the organization, we have all heard stories about those who have fallen into such excruciatingly uncomfortable professional situations. Jackie's story is such a case.

A talented and capable administrator, Jackie had built a solid reputation among colleagues, community members, and students as a committed and action-oriented leader. Within just a few years, he had become fully involved in his new college and community, demonstrating a love for innovation and change while helping his campus find its place on the national community college stage. He flourished while supporting the mission and goals of the institution and routinely accepted additional tasks "for the good of the order" without requesting additional compensation, since he realized resources were extremely tight.

In time, however, Jackie began to feel he was at the limit of his capacity for doing more or even properly fulfilling his existing commitments. In accepting an additional responsibility two years earlier, he had successfully built a unit that now needed the attention of a full-time administrator. Meanwhile, his original job responsibilities had also expanded, and he had lost some valuable members of his team because of his inability to garner support from his supervisor for compensating them adequately for the additional responsibilities that had fallen to them.

At the same time, Jackie sensed that his supervisor was doing less and less while accepting more than his fair share of praise and credit (as well as increased compensation) for the good things that were happening at the institution. When the time came to submit budget proposals for the coming year, Jackie outlined several options for dividing his responsibilities among one or more colleagues in order to create a more equitable situation. When the response from his supervisor was sternly negative, Jackie decided he had three options: accept the situation and make the best of it; go to his supervisor's supervisor to express his frustration; or walk away from the job because it was no longer rewarding.

Discussion Questions

1. Did Jackie accurately identify his options? Were there other, better options?

2. Were there any actions Jackie could have taken in earlier weeks and months to head off his feelings of frustration?

3. What else could have usefully been done at any point in this situation?

▪ Reflection

How to proceed when one's adamant beliefs are not shared by one's supervisor is an uncomfortable dilemma that requires serious reflective thought and consideration. Even when situations and relationships begin on a very positive note, they are vulnerable to deterioration if communications become slack. There are very few scenarios that justify breaking the chain of command, and such scenarios are precarious from every perspective. The rationale for jumping the chain of command must be that the supervisor's actions or intentions either contradict the mission and goals of the institution or otherwise jeopardize the general welfare. The chain of command is a sacred covenant that wise and ethical leaders respect, and burning bridges is a practice that they avoid.

Conclusion

Leaders emerge in all forms and at every level within an organization. Their comments, actions, and decisions have a profound effect on the future of individuals and the organization itself. Most would agree that there is no greater reward than simply making a difference, whether by guiding a single, struggling student, mentoring a bright young professional, or providing direction on a larger scale regarding an issue of institutional, state, or national concern. In every instance, the responsibilities and tasks of educational leaders are profoundly significant. When these responsibilities are carried out conscientiously, the rewards that come with leading from the head as well as the heart are well worth the effort.

References

Andrews, K. R. (1989, September/October). Ethics in practice. *Harvard Business Review, 67*(5), 99–104.

Bretz, R. D., & Judge, T. A. (1994). Person-organization fit and the theory of work adjustment: Implications for satisfaction, tenure, and career success. *Journal of Vocational Behavior, 44*(1), 32–54.

Caplan, R. D., & Van Harrison, R. (1993). Person-environment fit theory: Some history, recent developments, and future directions. *Journal of Social Issues, 49*(4), 253–275.

Starratt, R. J. (2005, Winter). Responsible leadership. *The Educational Forum, 69*(2), 124–133.

Stern, G. G. (1970). *People in context: Measuring person-environment congruence in education and industry.* New York, NY: Wiley.

11

Transformational Leadership and Ethical Dilemmas in Community Colleges

Sherry Stout-Stewart

Community colleges have led the way in allowing women to enter higher education as instructors, and community colleges are expected to lead the way in providing women with opportunities to attain senior leadership roles. An important nationwide topic in community college leadership is presidential succession, and some community colleges have initiated leadership academies to prepare future leaders to fill the anticipated leadership gap. Studies suggest that as women assume community college CEO positions, they will serve as transformational leaders and become leadership role models for women and men at community colleges and other institutions of higher learning.

In assuming community college CEO positions, women, as well as men and minorities, will face tough decisions. Many of these decisions will involve choosing between right and wrong, the easy, cut-and-dried decisions. The difficult decisions emerge when administrators are faced with ethical dilemmas: the choice between good and good or between right and right. During times of tough decision-making, some leaders rely on trusted colleagues or mentors for advice. Often, however, situations involving ethical dilemmas do not allow for extensive consultation or collaborative decision-making. Therefore, with the surge of new leaders and the change in leadership style that is expected in the next decade in the community college system, future leaders must prepare and equip themselves to be savvy problem-solvers.

The Anticipated Leadership Gap in Community College Leadership_____

Because of the number of senior administrators who are aging and projected to retire, the percentage of female community college presidents is expected to grow (Deitemeyer, 2002; Shults, 2001; Weisman & Vaughan, 2002). "An impending leadership crisis" is also predicted in the community college system because of the high number of retiring presidents, senior administrators, and faculty leaders (Shults, p. 1). Nevertheless, with the number of anticipated retirements in the next decade, female community college presidents are positioned to serve as change agents for leadership and become transformational leaders (Bell, 1995; Cooper, 1995; Twombly & Amey, 1994; DiCroce, 1995; Amey, 1999).

Community colleges are consistently described as interesting institutions for analyzing and studying women's leadership, as well as "the ideal setting for women presidents to redefine leadership, to have a positive impact on their institutions, in higher education, and society as a whole" (DiCroce, 1995, pp. 80–81; Stephenson, 2001; Tedrow, 2001). At the same time, community colleges, like many other contemporary organizations and institutions, have been characterized as "bureaucratic, hierarchical, and dominated by male and elite imagery" (Amey, 1999, p. 60). As for the pathway to the presidency, female community college presidents have experienced challenges in coping with personal and institutional hindrances during their ascension (Brown, 2000). Buddemeier (1998) found that 81% of all female presidents experienced sex discrimination on their path to the presidency.

As community college presidents retire, succeeding female presidents will help to fill the gap and serve as transformational leaders. In assuming these positions, female leaders will be faced with a myriad of challenges and dilemmas. Stephenson (2001) posits:

> As women leaders enter a new century, they are at a very difficult crossroad, a crossroad where public expectations, the demands of diverse populations, governmental scrutiny, and harsh financial realities intersect. . . . Not only would increasing numbers of women leaders have to deal directly with these issues, but the inclusion of women in leadership groups would enhance the resolution of these issues. (p. 193)

Resolving issues and having the ability to make decisions are essential to a leader's credibility. Giannini (2001) asserts, "Women must establish credibility by leading with commitment and following through" (pp. 210–211). Others, like Vaughan and Weisman (1998), have focused on the changes female leadership may bring about: "How female presidents differ from their male counterparts deserves special attention, for the experiences and attributes that women acquire in attaining and maintaining a presidency may be quite different from the experiences of men" (p. 23). The clear implication is that with the turnover in community college presidencies will come a transformation in leadership.

Transformational Leadership

According to Kouzes and Posner (2002), transformational leadership "occurs when, in their interactions, people 'raise one another to higher levels of motivation and morality'" (p. 153). According to this definition, transforming leadership "ultimately becomes moral in that it raises the level of human conduct and ethical aspiration of both the leader and the led, and thus it has transforming effects on both" (p. 153). In order to elevate human conduct and inspire others, specific leadership patterns and behaviors must be established, to aid in both making ethical decisions and confronting ethical dilemmas. Kouzes and Posner have identified five patterns of action in their Leadership Practices Inventory: challenge the process, inspire a shared vision, enable others to act, model the way, and encourage the heart.

A Nationwide Study of Female Community College Presidents

Composition of Female Community College Presidents

Community colleges are located in rural, urban, and suburban settings throughout the United States, as well as in American Samoa, Micronesia, Guam, the Marshall Islands, the Northern Mariana Islands, Palau, and Puerto Rico. The number of public, private, and tribal community colleges is 1,171 with varying enrollment figures. Thus, female community college presidents appear in institutions of differing sizes and cultural settings.

Female Community College Presidents' Perceptions of Effective Leadership: Leadership Practices and Behaviors (2004) is a nationwide study I conducted to determine the leadership patterns and behaviors of female CEOs in community college systems in rural, suburban, urban, and inner-city settings. Using the theory of transformational leadership and Kouzes and Posner's (2002) Leadership Practices Inventory, I determined that there were no significant differences in leadership habits as reported by female community college presidents of rural, suburban, urban, or inner-city settings. The results of the leadership patterns were ranked as follows by female community college presidents: enabling others to act, modeling the way, encouraging the heart, challenging the process, and inspiring a shared vision. According to Kouzes and Posner's percentile rankings, the performance ratings as reported by female community college presidents—that is, their perceptions of themselves—overall were considered high. With high percentile rankings on leadership patterns nationwide, leaders still have the task of solving problems in leadership roles and putting theory into practice.

Ethical Dilemmas

The necessity of addressing ethical dilemmas can build firm bridges between theory and practice. A leadership dilemma in most cases is best known as a situation in which there is no straightforward or simple course of action to follow. In other words, any decision will have disadvantages. What is needed therefore is the commitment to weigh the pros and to make a decision knowing the scales will not balance perfectly.

The Commitment of Community Colleges _____

Community college leaders, by design, are committed to educational values of community, excellence, honesty and integrity, teamwork, innovation, and staying on the cutting edge of technology. They value everyone and prove it with an open door. They strive for academic, professional, and personal bests. They treat each other with respect, civility, and fairness. They believe in the concept of teamwork, as well as global education. They provide learning opportunities in the areas of university transfer, general education, developmental education, workforce development, student development services, continuing education, community education, civic responsibility, and global education. Finally, community college leaders promote the concept of learning communities and are accountable to students and the community.

Putting Theory Into Practice: Real-World Applications _____

When theory and practice connect, the results are lessons learned from decisions. The following are situations that involve ethical dilemmas experienced by practitioners in the community college system. The purpose of outlining these particular scenarios is to provide future leaders with real-life examples that may help guide them in the future. In addition, these scenarios model ways to think about problems analytically and then make decisions that maximize integrity and fairness.

Sports Teams

After working hard to establish sports teams in the community college system, President McGrath finally received his wish of having basketball in the community college system on a state level. McGrath, his college, and the community eagerly awaited the first season. Being a former basketball player and coach, McGrath looked forward to the incorporation of sports into the system—in particular, the establishment of the first basketball team at his college—as part of his successful legacy as president.

The season passes, and President McGrath's team is playing for the conference championship and is favored to win. Then McGrath receives word from the vice president, who has been informed by the coach, that the players had a party after the previous night's game. Following this party, a female student alleged she was sexually assaulted by five of the star players. The media outlets have broken the story, campus protests have already begun, and President McGrath is under pressure to make a decision as to whether the team will continue to play in the conference championship. The players contend that they are all innocent and have submitted DNA samples, which will not be returned until after the conference championship. McGrath is faced with withdrawing his team from the tournament or allowing it to play on a probationary status. Furthermore, one of the accused players is a son of a member of the board of trustees.

What steps should President McGrath take in this situation? How should he justify his actions?

Separate Articulation Agreements

Having the best interests of the students in mind, President Coleman has worked out a separate articulation agreement with a local university. For two years, she had promoted and pitched this separate university articulation agreement to the students. The agreement states that students from Coleman's college who meet the transfer criteria, which include a 3.5 grade point average and an associate's degree, are to be automatically accepted to the local university.

It comes as a shock to President Coleman when nearly 150 students with college-transfer associate's degrees are not admitted for the semester. All of these students met the separate articulation requirements; some of the students exceeded them. Only about 20 were accepted into education and nursing programs, areas where graduates are in high demand.

The university president cites a space problem as the reason for the limitations. President Coleman responds that many of the community college students are nontraditional in many ways, including by needing to begin at the university on schedules other than the fall semester. Coleman also notes additional hardships, involving tax dependency, medical insurance coverage, and veteran's benefits, imposed on students who unexpectedly found themselves unable to enroll for the spring semester.

President Coleman is faced with the problem of students who were not accepted and how to handle the relationship with the university. If she discontinues the agreement, other students may not have this opportunity. If she continues the agreement, more students may not be accepted and may experience the same disappointment.

How could President Coleman handle this situation in a way that leaves open the best options and opportunities for her students?

Quid Pro Quo

As a college administrator managing a specialized industry training program, Vice President Jackson Elliott is approached by a company executive and asked to provide a certain training service. In exchange, the company executive offers to make a sizable contribution to the college's foundation. This particular company executive has a reputation of playing games with the rules. How Vice President Elliott responds to this request will determine the future working relationship with this particular company, and it will determine how he as an administrator will be perceived in the future. This particular company also employs a large number of the college's graduates.

What action should Elliott take in order to avoid present and future problems?

The Legislature, the Board of Trustees, and the Decision

President Hernandez learns at the Presidents' Association meeting that the members will vote on new placement test score recommendations. The current scores relied heavily on previous system workshops that involved developmental education, especially the culminating reports of a developmental education project. Also, a system-wide review of individual college test instruments, test scores, and implementation policies was conducted. There was no clear-cut majority score for any one course/test correlation.

The committee then consulted with the publishers of the major instruments. Based on nationally normed data, a score approximating the 50th percentile was chosen for each point of exit from a developmental course to the corresponding college-level course. These scores comprised the score portion of the original placement testing recommendations. Then the Placement Testing Validation Committee sought feedback from the instructional administrators, student personnel, and presidents. As a result, the State Board of Community Colleges approved the scores, which worked well for President Hernandez's college. The current scores have been used for years.

The proposed scores are lower than the current scores. When President Hernandez questioned the proposed scores, the rationale provided was that a Placement Testing Validation Committee worked from the following guiding principles:

- Current cut scores are fairly appropriate and need only refinement.

- Colleges want to optimize resources while providing developmental education for students who need it.

The committee chose the proposed scores based on their representing the lowest score at which there is no statistically significant decrease in the percent of students passing the first college-level course with a grade of C or higher.

President Hernandez informs the board of trustees at her college of the proposed test scores. She too seeks input from her vice presidents, deans, and faculty members. When Hernandez presents the proposed scores to her faculty, she finds that they are highly opposed to the proposed scores. She receives the following feedback:

- This is an issue that strongly affects admissions, counseling, curriculum, and financial aid.

- The current scores are working well for our students, especially our older students—a high percentage of our students are older due to numerous plant closings in the area.

- A change in the current scores will have a significant impact on transfer courses—not only could President Hernandez's college find itself having to offer additional transfer courses, it could also find an increased number of students unprepared for college-level work.

- The most severe impact of lower scores will be their negative effect on performance measures.

The presidents are to vote at the end of the month. President Hernandez presents all of this information to her board of trustees, which is in favor of the proposed scores because the state legislature is supporting them for budgetary reasons. The system office contends that the main reason for the proposed scores is that they will get students through programs faster and not keep them stuck in developmental courses. The final recommendations from the presidents to the state board of education will be based on a majority vote.

How should President Hernandez vote, and should she attempt to change this situation? If she attempts to change the situation, how should she proceed?

Conflict Resolution and Contract Renewals

Pam has been in her new position of dean for about a year, and she is also new to the area. Over the past year, she has inherited a couple of instructors who are arch rivals. Both are valued instructors with impeccable student evaluations and records of going far beyond the call of duty.

One of the instructors, Suzanne, teaches a course in a content area where there is a shortage of instructors. In addition, Suzanne's students have placed year after year in state and national competitions. The other instructor, Karen, is loved and adored by her students. Karen sponsors a club whose monthly events are eagerly anticipated by students, faculty, staff, and community members. Both instructors are constantly in the newspaper for their and their students' accomplishments. Both have also won awards for teaching excellence.

Pam is constantly visited by Suzanne and Karen. Each instructors complains to Pam about the other. She has talked to them separately and together, and she has used established conflict resolution techniques. They are both on action plans, and nothing seems to work. Last week, Pam was called to the break room and had to stand physically between the two during a heated argument. Not only is she receiving visits from Suzanne and Karen, but other instructors are also coming to voice their opinions about the two instructors. Some are dismayed by Suzanne's and Karen's lack of professionalism. Others are fueling the flames and seem to enjoy the action.

Pam learns from another instructor that Suzanne is married to a prominent and highly respected businessperson in the community, and Karen is the spouse of an influential politician. She also learns that Suzanne's spouse helped to campaign against Karen's spouse in the last election. The two couples have differing political agendas for the business community.

Pam has discussed this situation with the vice president, who has in turn discussed it with the president. The vice president has informed her that one of the instructors must not be renewed, and she must make the decision.

Which instructor should Pam renew and which should she not renew? How could she justify her decision?

Dilemmas and Discernment

Janyth Fredrickson is the new senior administrator in charge of instruction, and several heads of large academic divisions report to her. One of the division heads, who has many years of experience, is very supportive of her. This particular division head is willing to tackle new assignments and is eager to keep Dr. Fredrickson informed about the activities of the program areas and faculty within that division.

Some months later, as Dr. Fredrickson is getting to know the faculty and they are getting to know her, one of the faculty members approaches her unofficially and apologizes profusely for disappointing her. Perplexed by this statement, Dr. Fredrickson asks, "Disappointing me? About what?" The instructor replies that the division head had said Dr. Fredrickson was disappointed with the instructors and something they had done. Wanting to get information from the division head, Dr. Fredrickson replies in a diplomatic way and assures the instructor that all the instructors are valued and thanks the instructor for taking the initiative to talk to her.

Before Dr. Fredrickson can meet with the division head, faculty from two other programs within the division talk to her off the record about critical things they were told she had said. None of this information is true.

How should this situation be resolved, and who should be believed? Why?

The "Honeymoon Period" and Accreditation

John has been the vice president for instruction for one year, and he is close to the end of his "honeymoon period." He is aware that he is still defining for the college his set of standards and expectations.

Fortunately, the reaffirmation visit by the regional accrediting agency is seven years off. As is commonly known, one of the criteria the visiting team will check with great rigor is the academic preparation of the faculty and whether they have the degrees and courses required to teach in their fields.

By chance, John learns that several telecourses in one discipline have been taught in their entirety by an adjunct instructor for several years, even though a full-time instructor is listed as the instructor of record. The adjunct instructor is conscientious and well regarded but does not have appropriate academic credentials to teach in this area.

The explanation given by the department head is that the adjunct does a good job and that the formal class records indicate that a fully qualified instructor teaches the classes, even though this is not the case.

What should John do in this situation?

Keeping the Moral Compass

Lawrence Rouse receives an email from a county businessman who employs several hundred people. This employer operates several college training programs on campus and for years has made large contributions to the College Foundation. The email requested that a valued employee be given special consideration for admittance to the nursing program. The college's associate degree nursing program is very competitive, and the admissions process is based on receiving points for various preparatory coursework, tests, and experience. Students with the highest points are admitted on their merit. The employer is adamant regarding his desire for the employee to enter the program. There are other potential students who have higher scores and are qualified to enter the program according to the college's policies.

The employer contends that his employee has received the training she needs, and the college will, in turn, gain a qualified student. Further, he emphatically states that he will be helping a valued employee and wants to continue to enjoy a good relationship with the college.

How can Dr. Rouse keep the college in favor with the employer and keep his ethical compass pointed to fairness and honesty no matter what the consequences?

"Fix It"

The culture at a community college has long involved providing perks for members of the board of trustees. One long-standing perk was the trustees' practice of having their automobiles fixed by the automotive instructors (and not by the students) free of charge during the day or evening, week or weekend. The only charge to the trustees was for parts. Most trustees, however, had discontinued this practice, and when a new president, Dr. Smith, is hired, only one trustee was still requesting consideration with his automobile.

The automotive instructors talked with Dr. Smith and expressed their concern about being asked to spend classroom time fixing the trustee's automobile. Dr. Smith asked the instructors to devise a policy that would address employee and citizen use of the college's automotive services. She then met with the trustee and explained that auditors were looking at situations where employees or trustees received benefits by virtue of their positions, and that one of the community colleges in the state had been cited in the state auditor's report for giving preferential treatment to the president when the automotive department fixed his car without the service being related to instruction or being performed by students in the program. Dr. Smith further explained that the college would no longer be able to fix the trustee's car unless the service fell within the guideline that the automotive program developed. The trustee accepted the explanation, and the board is to approve a college-wide policy on the use of automotive services at its summer retreat.

As a new president, how should Dr. Smith present the new college-wide policy once it is approved?

The Open Door and Discipline

According to Randy Young, vice president for instruction and student development, determining student disciplinary actions puts administrators in ethical dilemmas. When an administrator decides to take action that will lead to a student being expelled or suspended from the college, it usually involves considerable reflection and weighing of all possible options. Of course, there are extreme situations that do not create such dilemmas.

When a student's behavior is obviously dangerous and detrimental to other students and the college, an administrator has no choice but to take serious action against the student.

There is a broad range of student behaviors whereby the appropriate response is not so clear-cut. When considering student infractions, an administrator must carefully weigh the possible damage to the college by allowing the student to continue classes against the effect on the student of being suspended or expelled. Most often, such a student is marginal academically, behaviorally, and/or psychologically. By allowing students to continue to attend college, an administrator may be preventing them from becoming "lost to society." However, their behavior may be such that an administrator needs to demonstrate to the other students that certain behaviors will not be tolerated. These situations cause administrators to pause and think at some point, "What will eventually happen to these students without the structure of college in their lives?" This decision-making process is often compounded when parents and counselors become involved.

Ethically, how does a community college administrator deal with marginal students in a fair and consistent manner and ensure a safe and orderly environment? Taking into consideration fairness, ethical dilemmas, and the open-door policy of a community college, how would an administrator write a code of conduct for his or her college?

Conclusion

With the number of projected retirements in the community college system, many women will inevitability assume the role of CEO, in many cases for the first time. Because of this coming trend, the next decade will be an unprecedented era nationwide for redefining leadership in the community college system. Many female community college presidents already perceive themselves as transformational leaders.

Leading with commitment and having the ability to make decisions and support those decisions are the trademarks of effective and successful leaders. They prepare for the seemingly no-win situations. They learn from the experiences of others as well as from their own experiences. They learn the art of how to connect theory and practice. Finally, I believe community colleges will continue to be interesting contexts in which to study leadership, because community college leaders, women and men, have to deal with every major issue in higher education.

Author Note

I wish to thank the following people for sharing their suggestions and input for this chapter: Janyth Fredrickson, Deborah Lamm, Lawrence Rouse, Randy Young, and Jackson Elliott.

References

Amey, M. J. (1999). Navigating the raging river: Reconciling issues of identity, inclusion, and administrative practice. In K. M. Shaw, J. R. Valadez, & R. A. Rhoads (Eds.), *Community colleges as cultural texts: Qualitative explorations of organizational and student culture* (pp. 59–82). Albany, NY: State University of New York Press.

Bell, C. S. (1995). "If I weren't involved with schools, I might be radical": Gender consciousness in context. In D. M. Dunlap & P. A. Schmuck (Eds.), *Women leading in education* (pp. 288–312). Albany, NY: State University of New York Press.

Brown, T. M. (2000). *Female presidents of selected independent colleges: Career paths, profiles, and experiences.* Unpublished doctoral dissertation, North Carolina State University.

Buddemeier, S. (1998). *Female community college presidents: Career paths, experiences, and perceptions of the presidency* (Doctoral dissertation, North Carolina State University, 1998). *Dissertation Abstracts International, 59*(03), 744.

Cooper, J. E. (1995). Administrative women and their writing: Reproduction and resistance in bureaucracies. In D. M. Dunlap & P. A. Schmuck (Eds.), *Women leading in education* (pp. 235–246). Albany, NY: State University of New York Press.

Deitemeyer, K. (2002). *The community college presidency for the 21st century: Female leadership for higher education.* Unpublished doctoral dissertation, University of South Florida.

DiCroce, D. (1995). Women and the community college presidency: Challenges and possibilities. In B. K. Townsend (Ed.), *New directions for community colleges: No. 89. Gender and power in the community college* (pp. 79–88). San Francisco, CA: Jossey-Bass.

Giannini, S. T. (2001, March). Future agendas for women community college leaders and change agents. *Community College Journal of Research and Practice, 25*(3), 201–211.

Kouzes, J. M., & Posner, B. Z. (2002). *The leadership challenge* (3rd ed.). San Francisco, CA: Jossey-Bass.

Shults, C. (2001). *The critical impact of impending retirements on community college leadership* (Research Brief No. 1). Washington, DC: Community College Press.

Stephenson, G. W. (2001, March). Women as community college leaders. *Community College Journal of Research and Practice, 25*(3), 193–200.

Stout-Stewart, S. (2004). *Female community college presidents' perceptions of effective leadership: Leadership practices and behaviors.* Unpublished doctoral dissertation, University of North Carolina–Chapel Hill.

Tedrow, B. (2001). Three general patterns typify women's leadership styles. In M. D. Wenniger & M. H. Conroy (Eds.), *Gender equity or bust! On the road to campus leadership with* Women in Higher Education (pp. 17–20). San Francisco, CA: Jossey-Bass.

Twombly, S. B., & Amey, M. J. (1994). Leadership skills for participative governance. In G. A. Baker, III (Ed.), *A handbook on the community college in America: Its history, mission, and management* (pp. 268–283). Westport, CT: Greenwood Press.

Vaughan, G. B., & Weisman, I. M. (1998). *Community college presidency at the millennium.* Washington, DC: Community College Press.

Weisman, I. M., & Vaughan, G. B. (2002). *The community college presidency 2001* (Research Brief No. 3). Washington, DC: Community College Press.

12

Presidential Support for Civic Engagement and Leadership Education

Louis S. Albert

In the process of deciding on the focus of this chapter, I wrote a column in my campus newsletter asking for suggestions about how to approach the subject of ethical leadership in the community college. From the many suggestions I received, three themes emerged.

The first theme revolved around the far-too-frequent news about ethical breaches, scandals, and legal transgressions on the part of corporate executives, representatives of the news media, and politicians. Stories about the illegal use of corporate resources, "cooking the books," bribes, and extravagant compensation packages have made front-page news at both the national and local levels. That news, and sadly more than a few similar stories coming from the higher education sector, led my colleagues to suggest that I reflect on the implications of these unethical behaviors for executive leadership in community colleges. What does being "beyond reproach" really mean? How can we model behavior that sets the highest ethical standard for the organizational units that report to us as executive administrators? When we "do the right thing," what does this communicate to our students? When we do the wrong thing, what does *that* communicate?

The second theme came from faculty and staff suggestions that I reflect on recent reports from all sectors of education (K–12 and higher education) about faculty and staff speaking out on controversial social issues.

In some cases, such outspoken academics have become lightning rods for heated national debates, and college presidents have been caught in the middle. In 2005, for example, University of Colorado Professor of Ethnic Studies Ward Churchill made some highly controversial statements about the underlying causes of the September 11, 2001, attacks on the Pentagon and World Trade Center. Churchill's speeches made national news, as did questions about his academic credentials. Political leaders criticized both Churchill and University of Colorado policies, particularly policies associated with the award of tenure to members of the faculty. The University of Colorado leadership and especially its president were frequent subjects of print and broadcast media reports on the Churchill story.

While we in the academy cherish the long-standing value of academic freedom, legislatures and taxpayers tend to look at academic freedom through a different lens. Like it or not, as executive administrators, we are often asked to take positions on highly sensitive public issues. The questions are obvious: What is the appropriate balance between academic freedom and our responsibility as educators to the public that supports us? What is our role as executive leaders in maintaining that balance? And, as asked earlier, what do our students learn from our responses?

The third theme is the one that caught my attention, with its focus on the teaching and learning process. Those who advocated this approach recommended that I reflect on how we can better organize the undergraduate experience so that student learning outcomes include developing responsible citizens and ethical leaders, both in the workplace and in the communities they call home. Faculty and staff in this instance strongly suggested that community college presidents must not only model the highest standards of ethical leadership, and not only be prepared to speak out in a fair and balanced way about controversial social issues, but also support programs that extend their ethical commitments to embrace the education of the next generation of ethical leaders for our communities and our nation.

Beyond Workforce Development: Educating Citizens and Leaders

In January 2000, the W. K. Kellogg Foundation published a landmark monograph, edited by Alexander Astin and Helen Astin, titled *Leadership Reconsidered: Engaging Higher Education in Social Change.* In the opening chapter, the Astins write:

> The problems that plague American society are, in many respects, problems of leadership. By "leadership" we mean not only what elected and appointed public officials do, but also the critically important civic work performed by those individual citizens who are actively engaged in making a positive difference in the society. A leader, in other words, can be anyone—regardless of formal position— who serves as an effective social change agent. In this sense, every faculty member and staff member, not to mention every student, is a potential leader. (p. 2)

As educators, we are in the leadership development business, even when we do not pay explicit attention to the process. But sadly that is not what our students think. Ask almost any college student, especially community college students, why they are in school, and only a handful will talk about learning how to be leaders. Most will instead say something about obtaining the knowledge and skills needed to be competitive in the workplace. Most students tend to equate "learning with earning," and with good reason: College graduates do earn more than those without a college degree. And community college students have the added incentive of being able to obtain the knowledge and skills needed for gainful employment in a relatively short time, through two-year associate degree programs and certificate programs that can be completed in under one year.

A growing number of educators understand that preparation for gainful employment and preparation for future leadership roles at work and in the community need not be mutually exclusive outcomes of undergraduate education. Helping students understand that workforce skills and leadership development can and should be simultaneous outcomes of college is our challenge as presidents, as administrative staff, and as faculty members. Responding to that challenge provides rich opportunities for presidents to align their commitments as ethical leaders with actions that demonstrate those commitments.

Public expectations for preparing a workforce that is highly competent and highly ethical are growing. Without question, workforce and economic development will continue to be high priorities for community colleges; employers, students, and the larger community expect that of us. But those same constituents also expect community colleges to develop program initiatives like service-learning and leadership training programs that help students become engaged and socially responsible citizens and leaders. Responding to those expectations and supporting meaningful civic learning and leadership development programs should also be high priorities for community college presidents. When preparation for both work and engaged citizenship are components of the undergraduate experience, it benefits students, employers, and the community. As ethical leaders, we should have both at the top of our presidential priority list.

Advocating for the Civic Mission of Higher Education

Organizations like Campus Compact and the faculty-based disciplinary societies have become advocates for the civic mission of higher education and for preparing the graduates of our institutions to be engaged and responsible citizens. The disciplinary societies have promoted these goals through discipline-specific publications and initiatives, and most now offer sessions and workshops on service-learning and related concepts at their national and regional conferences.

Campus Compact is a consortium of nearly 1,000 college and university presidents committed to advancing the civic mission of colleges and universities. Through the consortium's vision statement, Compact presidents are very clear about that civic mission:

> Campus Compact envisions colleges and universities as vital agents and architects of a diverse democracy, committed to educating students for responsible citizenship in ways that both deepen their learning and improve the quality of community life. We challenge all of higher education to make civic and community engagement an institutional priority. (Campus Compact, 2006)

The growth of Campus Compact as a consortium speaks volumes about the rapid development of the civic engagement movement in higher education. Moreover, community colleges are significant players in that movement, with more than 200 consortium presidents representing two-year colleges. In 1999, Campus Compact drafted the *Presidents' Declaration on the Civic Responsibility of Higher Education*. The signatories to the declaration stated:

How can we realize this vision of institutional public engagement? It will take as many forms as there are types of colleges and universities. And it will require our hard work, as a whole and within each of our institutions. We will know we are successful by the robust debate on our campuses, and by the civic behaviors of our students. We will know it by the civic engagement of our faculty. We will know it when our community partnerships improve the quality of community life and the quality of the education we provide...

We believe that the challenge of the next millennium is the renewal of our own democratic life and reassertion of social stewardship. In celebrating the birth of our democracy, we can think of no nobler task than committing ourselves to helping analyze and lead a national movement to reinvigorate the public purposes and civic mission of higher education. We believe that now and through the next century, our institutions must be vital agents and architects of a flourishing democracy. (Campus Compact, 1999, p. 3)

The scope of the civic engagement movement is also evidenced by the large numbers of students, faculty, and staff who participate in service-learning, volunteer service, leadership development, and other forms of civic engagement. In 2003, Campus Compact estimated the total number of students engaged in service on member campuses exceeded 1.7 million. Additionally, more than 22,000 faculty on member campuses were involved in service-learning or related activities (Campus Compact, 2004).

Toward a Next Generation of Ethical Leaders: What Community College Presidents Should Do_____

As higher education professionals, we are in a powerful position to do something about the quality of civic life in our communities, our nation, and even the world. But presidential leadership is critical if our efforts are going to have maximum impact. The credibility of these efforts will be greatly enhanced if presidents commit to the following:

- Consistent and visible public actions that reflect the highest standards of personal ethical behavior

- Consistent and visible public actions with respect to the administrative leadership teams that report to the president, and expectations that the members of those leadership teams take similar consistent and visible public actions

- Consistent and visible public dialogue with faculty leaders on issues of ethical responsibility and behavior

- Commitment to organizing opportunities for students to understand and exercise ethical standards as workers and participants in our democracy

When presidents take the ethical high road in a consistent and visible manner, students learn from that behavior. Taking the ethical high road, however, is not only about doing the right thing; it also means supporting programs and services that enable students to grow as responsible citizens and ethical leaders. Here is a starter list:

- Become a public advocate for the civic mission of higher education. Join other presidents in an advocacy role by becoming a member of Campus Compact.

- Underwrite the creation of a service-learning center that provides support for faculty and students wishing to combine academic study, community-service activities, and reflection so that the quality of learning is deepened and the quality of community service is enhanced.

- Establish leadership development initiatives and expand opportunities for leadership development education beyond student government and honors programs to the general student population.

- Encourage all occupational program faculty members to include professional ethics and leadership components in their courses.

- Encourage all faculty to include issues of civic responsibility, ethics, and leadership in their courses.

- Include opportunities for civic learning and leadership development in the cocurriculum, and include opportunities for student volunteer service. Create linkages between these co-curricular activities and academic service-learning activities.

- Create partnerships between the college, local K–12 institutions, and community agencies that provide opportunities for college students to mentor younger students in both academic skills and civic learning. To the extent possible, coordinate college and K–12 service-learning and volunteer service activities.

- Encourage and support staff efforts to provide volunteer services to the community. Publicly recognize faculty and staff who provide these services.

- Talk to the community about these civic learning and leadership development initiatives. Tell them what the college is doing and why it is important. Be sure that the public understands this is one of the college's highest priorities.

Leadership and Service: An International Perspective

Adel Safty is the UNESCO Leadership Chair and founding president of the School of Government and Leadership at the University of Bahcesehir in Turkey. For the past seven years, he and I have served together on the board of the International Partnership for Service-Learning and Leadership, an organization that provides opportunities for both undergraduate and graduate students from around the world to engage in academic study and service in 15 countries. When Safty joined the board in 1997, he immediately saw the connection between service and leadership development and encouraged the board to add the word *leadership* to the organization's name. Writing in *Knowing and Doing: The Theory and Practice of Service-Learning* (2005), Safty states:

> There is a real need for a new conception of leadership. . . .
> The new multicultural and multidimensional conception
> of leadership would be one that is related to good gover-
> nance, good management, and multilateral cooperation.
> Whether it is at the local, national, regional, or interna-
> tional level, whether it is in the political arena, in the mar-
> ketplace, in civil society institutions, in the academy, in

the public or private sector, we need leaders motivated by moral convictions and sustained commitment to human development. Leadership will thus have been democratized. (p. 129)

Safty's prescription for what he refers to as the "democratization of leadership" proposes intensified efforts at international leadership training programs. The kinds of leadership Safty is calling for and the kinds of leadership skills community college students can gain through participation in local service-learning and leadership development activities are remarkably similar. What both efforts need are commitment and support from presidents who model high ethical leadership standards and who are consistent and public in their support for these efforts.

Conclusion

Community college presidents must exemplify the highest forms of professional and ethical behavior. The message from elected officials, community leaders, faculty, staff, and students is very clear: They want their presidents to be models of ethical behavior. The message from presidents to their faculty, staff, and students must be equally clear: Ethical presidents must expect ethical behavior and be prepared to take strong action when college employees or students step over the line ethically.

Ethical presidents also have an obligation to make wise use of college resources to improve the quality of life in the communities they serve, to indeed develop their communities through learning. What kind of learning? Learning that is long lasting and meaningful, whether directed toward vocational skills or preparation for further study; learning that is relevant; and learning that pays attention to the student as both a future productive member of the workforce and an ethical and responsible citizen. Educating future citizen-leaders for our American democracy may indeed be our highest calling.

References

Astin, A. W., & Astin, H. S. (2000). *Leadership reconsidered: Engaging higher education in social change*. Battle Creek, MI: Kellogg Foundation.

Campus Compact. (1999). *Presidents' declaration on the civic responsibility of higher education*. Providence, RI: Author.

Campus Compact. (2004). *Season of service: Campus Compact's annual report for fiscal year 2003–2004*. Providence, RI: Campus Compact.

Campus Compact. (2006). *Campus Compact vision statement*. Retrieved December 1, 2006, from www.compact.org/about/

Safty, A. (2005). Leadership democratized. In L. A. Chisholm (Ed.), *Knowing and doing: The theory and practice of service-learning* (pp. 117–137). New York, NY: IPSL Press.

13

A Guide to Ethical Decision-Making by Presidents and Boards

Gary W. Davis

"I find that the three major administrative problems on a campus are sex for the students, athletics for the alumni and parking for the faculty."

In that whimsical statement, former University of California president Clark Kerr acknowledged that colleges represent more than one value system. When values within a college collide, presidents and boards often find themselves in the middle of the collision. Each college constituency expects the president and the board to sympathize with its point of view. Not realizing how conflicted a college can be, the general public expects presidents and trustees to be able to articulate what the college stands for. Faced with a variety of expectations, college presidents and boards need to know how to sort through diverse perspectives and issues in order to make sound ethical decisions.

This chapter provides a method for ethical decision-making by boards and presidents. The terms *ethics* and *morality* derive from roots meaning "common practice." Yet controversies swirling around colleges and universities in the 21st century make it clear that sometimes "common practices" are unacceptable. Although binge drinking and casual sexual relationships (sometimes between faculty and students) might be common in today's colleges, they are a matter of concern for many. Every fall brings news stories of students who die after drinking to excess. Even given the fact that faculty-student liaisons have been known since the days of Plato's Academy, many condemn such relationships as abuse of a "power relationship." When colleges take large contributions from those who have operated on the edge of the law and socially accepted norms, the institutions expose themselves to criticism. Whenever those in higher education fail to provide career preparation or a reasonable chance of graduation to their students, colleges are faulted for failing to meet their responsibility to students.

Ethical challenges are not reserved for college presidents. What should a board of trustees do if it suspects its president of falsifying enrollment reports? What is the board's responsibility for members who double dip on their board expense reports? How should a board balance the interests of alumni against the views of the general public during a controversy over the college's Native American mascot? Each of these situations is real. Each has occurred within the past three years. In such cases, the president and the board are usually left to deal with the ethical dilemma on their own and without the help of reliable precedent or generally accepted standards of conduct.

The stakes are high. Shattered reputations create problems for organizations whose leaders exhibit unethical behavior. The 2004 Cone Corporate Citizenship Study, notes Jacklyn Boice (2005), shows that Americans do not tolerate organizations whose leaders act unethically. Ninety percent of Americans would consider switching their loyalty away from an organization whose leaders exhibit unethical or illegal behavior; 81% would speak out against the organization among family and friends; 75% would refuse to work for the organization; and 67% of the organization's employees would be "less than loyal" to the organization. The study reveals that organizations are now evaluated in terms of a "triple bottom line" that measures their performance financially and in terms of the organization's treatment of its environment and its contribution to society.

Many CEOs are investigated or fired for their financial failures. Many others lose their jobs because of "matters as modest as handling business expense accounts" (Browning, 2005, p. 56). Contrary to those who trivialize ethics by reverting to a simplistic "front page" or "sniff" test, distinguishing what is ethical is not always easy. Is it unethical for a professor to require students to buy her textbook? Should college presidents be reimbursed for travel that combines business with pleasure? Should the president limit his consulting income in order to be certain that the college is well led? To what degree should the president be an agent of social change when such activity takes a toll on private contributions to the college? What does the president owe the board that hired her?

Like their presidents, board members regularly face daunting ethical challenges. Is it ethical to raise tuition when the college reserves stand at record levels? Is it ethical for a college to pay its part-time instructors less than a living wage? Is it better to employ part-time faculty at a low salary or to deny students sections of courses they need to complete their studies? Should the college purchase expensive hybrid vehicles when to do so puts pressure on student tuition rates? Is it ethical for a college to convert a critical wetland for the location of a new, badly needed classroom building? Should the college spend money to redress the consequences of social evils like slavery that it had no role in creating? Is it wrong to hire a contractor who is related to a board member when that contractor is the only locally available source of the needed service? What does a board owe the person it hires as the college president?

The New Expeditions project of the Association of Community College Trustees and the American Association of Community Colleges found that unethical behavior was one of the top seven failures of college trustees:

> When the public perceives that a trustee is benefiting from a conflict of interest, governance and the college suffer. . . . Ethical conflicts will continue until boards adopt systematic measures to alert their members to ethical compromises in the making. Boards also need help exploring leadership and core values. Many trustees have never had an opportunity to explore ethical dilemmas and the techniques of ethical decision making. (Davis, 2000)

In order to help trustees and presidents lead ethically, I present in this chapter a series of ethical questions that boards and presidents can use. Many presidents and trustees will recognize the origin of the questions: They come from Rotary International's Four-Way Test and from the well-known Serenity Prayer. Because presidents and trustees will already be familiar with the questions, they will be able to remember and use them during the course of their deliberations.

1. Is this something that ought to be changed?

"To change"

Although Alcoholics Anonymous made the Serenity Prayer famous, it was originally written by one of America's greatest 20th-century philosophers, Reinhold Niebuhr. Raised in the small town of Lincoln, Illinois, Professor Niebuhr was a Lutheran pastor from Detroit when he was called to Union Theological Seminary in New York to teach ethics. A renowned teacher and lecturer, the bilingual Niebuhr published a series of weighty books and essays, and despite his German roots, he was instrumental in challenging Christian pacifism during the early years of World War II.

His longest-lasting contribution to American thought, however, was his "Serenity Prayer," which most of us have heard in one form or another. In the prayer, Niebuhr expresses the hope that he will be able to discern the things that ought to be changed; he asks for courage to take on the task of setting right the wrongs that can be corrected; moreover, he asks for the patience to accept the things that cannot be changed. Here is the first and most often-quoted part of the Serenity Prayer:

> God grant me the serenity
> to accept the things I cannot change;
> courage to change the things I can;
> and wisdom to know the difference.

The Serenity Prayer begins by asking for ethical sensitivity. What ought to be changed? Although some believe ethical decisions occur only rarely in the work of a president or a board of trustees, the Serenity Prayer suggests that every time a board or a president strives to improve a college, ethical decisions are in play. Presidents and boards try to change a college because something good is missing and ought to be supplied or because something is wrong and needs to be eliminated. When boards try to increase the enrollment of underrepresented groups, they are trying to right a wrong. When presidents try to discourage irresponsible drinking by the college's students, they are trying to make things better. At their very root, both efforts result from ethical decision-making.

When boards and presidents ask, "What ought to be changed?" they are not denying the essential goodness of the college. Rather, they are striving for excellence. Not satisfied with what Garrison Keillor has called the "pretty good," boards and presidents want the college to be continuously improving. In so doing, they are responding to the first question suggested by the Serenity Prayer: "What ought to be changed?"

2. Is this something we can change?

■ *"To change the things I can"*

Although there is a school of ethical thinking that disavows the importance of consequences in ethical decision-making, few trustees and presidents have the luxury of ignoring results. They simply do not have time to tilt at windmills. Instead, they must focus their energy on projects that have some realistic chance of success. College presidents and boards are judged by the results they produce. Thus, one of the first questions that presidents and trustees must ask themselves about an ethical issue is, "Can we do something about this?"

Some challenges are beyond the grasp of presidents and boards. One is the friction that free academic inquiry produces. Parents of college freshmen often ask presidents, "Why are you challenging my child's values, the values that we taught our children when they were small?" In the fourth century B.C.E., Socrates was put to death for "corrupting the youth." Of course, Socrates said he was only teaching the youth to think for themselves, and academicians have used the same defense ever since. Unless they wish to reverse the academy's long-standing tradition of academic freedom, presidents and trustees must admit that they cannot remove the pain that comes with intellectual growth. Just as King Canute could not turn back the tide in the English legend, neither can a board of trustees or a college president guarantee that students will be returned to their families with minds and spirits unchanged.

On the other hand, some problems can be solved. Presidents and trustees do have many opportunities to recognize and rectify problematic situations. If abuses are occurring in the athletic department of a college, the president can require the athletic director to correct the abuses. As the Myles Brand/Bobby Knight conflict at Indiana University showed, correcting abuses is not always easy on the president or the board of trustees. Sometimes a price must be paid. So, those who decide to act in order to make the college a better place must ask themselves a second question. In order to find what needs to be changed in the college, trustees would be well advised to focus on the results that the institution is producing. Is there any evidence that the students are learning? How has the college improved their lives? In what ways is the community better off because of what the students have learned? When feedback to the board reveals problems within the college, the board can ask the president to address the problems and report back to the board. When the president requires additional resources to rectify the situation, the board is obligated to find those resources. As long as the college has the capacity to right its wrongs, the board and the president have an ethical obligation to try.

3. Do I have the courage to do the right thing?

■ *"Courage to change the things I can"*

Some believe that in the end, good actions are always rewarded. The evidence for such a position, however, is lacking. Socrates, Jesus, Abraham Lincoln, and Martin Luther King all paid with their lives. All were tested in their final hours, and all passed the test because they had developed and measured their courage before it was required of them. The time to ask about one's own level of courage is well before the courage is required. That is why Marine Corps infantry training is so rigorous. Marines are taught that much will be required of them—more than many recruits first thought they had the ability to give. But one need not be a Marine in order to understand the need for self-understanding. In his best-selling series of books, *What Color Is Your Parachute?*, Richard Bolles (2006) advises people to figure out who they are now instead of waiting until times of crisis. Once our courage quotient is understood and acknowledged, we will be prepared to do the right thing, even though standing for what is right may require serious sacrifices.

Before the fat is in the fire, each board and president should take some time for introspection. What does a person value, and what does he or she believe in? For what values and causes would a person be willing to sacrifice much of what he or she has? Now is the time to review the courageous acts of some great predecessors. Some are embellished with humor and the benefit of substantial reflection. For example, in recounting his stand on behalf of free speech (and his subsequent 1967 firing by then-governor Ronald Reagan), former University of California president Clark Kerr said that he ended his career in the UC system the way he started it: "fired with enthusiasm." In his latter years, Kerr coauthored *The Guardians* (1989), a volume on the importance of courageous trustees that is still a useful reference for community college presidents and trustees. With his coauthor

Marian Gade, Kerr also published a study of character in American college presidents: *The Many Lives of Academic Presidents: Time, Place, and Character* (1986).

4. Can I find a way to live with what cannot be changed?

■ *"To accept the things I cannot change"*

As many Europeans under Nazi occupation during World War II discovered, sometimes life demands more than an ounce of stoicism. When a bad situation cannot be changed, those who must endure it can control their responses to it. As a member of the French underground, Jean-Paul Sartre wrote and produced a modern version of Sophocles's *Antigone* in order to remind the French that everyone knew the German occupation was unjust. When a morally troubling situation exists and we are powerless to change it, we can at the very least acknowledge the problems it creates for us. In so doing, we nurture and sustain our own values. By resisting the urge to lash out at a situation that is clearly beyond our capacity to alter, we preserve our resources to fight another day. Having what Neibuhr calls "the wisdom to know the difference" between situations we can change and those we cannot makes all the difference in the long run.

5. What's the truth?

■ *"Is it the truth?"—from the Four-Way Test*

Under the influence of advertising, today's leaders have developed a disturbing tendency to ignore the truth. Contemporary society seems to be driven by the notion that as long as people believe in something or somebody, the question of truthfulness is secondary, if not irrelevant. There is no doubt that people often act on their beliefs even when they have little supporting evidence for their convictions. Convictions do not require inquiry into truth. The American philosopher William James even argued that truth is what works, and those who accept James's arguments believe that the search for truth should take a backseat to experimentation. Yet scientists know that well-conceived experiments are those that test a hypothesis that is supported by what scientists already know. Scientific knowledge builds on previous discoveries, and those discoveries are supported by evidence. In science, truth counts.

Those who ignore the importance of truth run the risk of creating a house of cards that can collapse at any moment, to the great peril of all those who dwell within. The Third Reich was an example of a belief system that was founded without regard to truth. For the Nazi theorists who hijacked science, the purity of one's beliefs trumped every other consideration. For a while the system worked, and European nations fell one by one to the fantasy-driven Nazi leadership. Yet, in the end, the Nazi beliefs proved false and the system imploded.

Everyone who has experienced the dawning of truth knows how irritating its arrival can be. The truth often upsets previous beliefs. It throws leaders off balance and upends conventional wisdom. For all those reasons, there is a human tendency to ignore or hide truth when it becomes inconvenient. Herbert Taylor, the author of the Rotarian "Four-Way Test," knew how discomforting truth could be when his cookware advertising department put before him a campaign that proclaimed his aluminum pots and pans "the greatest cookware in the world." Taylor knew that the claim was false, and he rejected the advertising campaign, even though the rejection put his position in the company in jeopardy. Taylor knew that eventually the truth would come out and that any gain obtained by temporarily disguising the truth would ultimately backfire. He knew that his company would gain more by attending to the truth than by bending it.

College presidents and boards face the same challenge. When an institution's vaunted program comes up short, college leaders are inclined to hide the bad news. Colleges sometimes find that their placement rates are disappointing or that their transfer students have not succeeded in their new institutions. Because many college board meetings are required to be held in public, most presidents and boards are inclined not to put instances of their institution's failures on the board's agenda. As a result, board meetings are dominated by "happy talk" in hopes that the public will be persuaded of the college's value to society. The problem with positive spin, of course, is that ultimately the truth will come out, and then the leaders who failed to recognize and share it will be seen as frauds. Presidents and trustees must be able to tell the truth even when it hurts.

6. What decisions are fair to all concerned?

▪ *"Is it fair to all concerned?"—from the Four-Way Test*

The second Rotarian test measures the fairness of decisions to those who have a stake in the outcome. The first challenge here is to be able to identify all the stakeholders. It is a fact that very often one or more of those concerned are overlooked. The tendency for most people is to consider only those who are directly involved at the moment the decision is made. The folly of such an analysis is easy to see. When two people decide to marry, each is involved in the decision and its outcome. But many others are involved as well. The parents and other family of the couple will be affected by their decision. Should they have children, the couple's offspring will be affected. On reflection, the range of people affected by the seemingly simple decision of two persons to marry is easy to see. But reflection is required.

When the value of a college program is measured, it is often measured against the cost of the tuition the student pays. Yet tuition covers only a fraction of the total operating budget of a public college. Most of the freight is paid by financial aid programs, college donors, and taxpayers. In evaluating programs, college leaders must consider more than the student who benefits directly; they must also consider the other parties who pay for the programs. Trustees ought to ask: "Do the program's results meet the expectations of the college's donors and others who have made the student's enrollment possible?"

The Four-Way Test asks whether those involved have been treated fairly. Fairness is achieved when arbitrary treatment is avoided and each receives his or her due. This does not mean everyone is treated fairly or that everyone receives the same benefit, but it does mean the rules for participation are worked out ahead of time and observed. It also means that each receives what is appropriate. There is no doubt that the primary recipients of a college's benefits are the students, but the students' families and future employers are owed some benefit as well. Does the college define a role for those who are not students, and are those other college participants informed of the role they can play? Is their right to play the role that is assigned to them protected by the college? Do all of the college's stakeholders receive their due? These are questions that boards and presidents ought to address regularly.

7. What decisions build goodwill and better friendships?

■ *"Will it build goodwill and better friendships?"*
—from the Four-Way Test

According to Doug Smith,

> Organizations are not just places where people have jobs. They are our neighborhoods, our communities. They are where we join with other people to make a difference for others and ourselves. If we think of them only as the places where we have jobs, we not only lose the opportunity for meaning, but we endanger the planet. (qtd. in Hammonds, 2004, p. 67)

Smith argues persuasively that while Americans' lives were once centered in a geographical place, today they are centered in our organizations and institutions: "It is in markets, organizations, and networks . . . that you spend your time, pursue your most pressing purposes, and find meaning in your life" (p. 67). With a sufficient degree of ethical know-how, an organization can build goodwill.

A story involving Four-Way Test author Herbert Taylor illustrates the point. After Taylor's company, Club Aluminum, awarded a printing contract, the lowest bidder came to Taylor and told him that he had miscalculated his bid by $500. He asked Taylor to increase the price that the Club Aluminum Company would pay. Taylor knew that he could hold the printer to his bid, but he decided to cover the additional $500 cost. He said he decided to help the printer because it would be the fair thing to do. Of course, it also built goodwill within the Chicago business community. Taylor's selfless act, undertaken at some considerable risk to his own company, set a tone of mutual respect and concern among the companies of Chicago. In so doing, it increased the level of trust that companies had for one another. Trust and goodwill then functioned as a lubricant in future business dealings. When business officials trusted one another, they were willing to go the extra mile in the expectation that a favor extended could someday be returned. They were not disappointed.

8. What solutions are beneficial to all concerned?

▪ *"Will it be beneficial to all concerned?"—from the Four-Way Test*

"People want [organizations] to conduct business in a way that benefits everyone concerned," asserts Jacklyn Boice (2005, p. 25). The fourth Rotarian test of ethical behavior asks, "Will it be beneficial to all concerned?" The test seems simple enough, but in actual practice people frequently overlook stakeholders. For example, decision-makers often forget the effect that the decision will have on those who might face similar dilemmas in the future. In other words, situations involve not only current stakeholders, but also those who might be affected by the precedent the decision establishes. Similarly, decisions sometimes affect those who preceded the current decision-makers. If previous generations of trustees sacrificed in order to establish the voters' confidence in the board's stewardship, a spendthrift decision by today's board dishonors the college's previous trustees, a group that might easily be overlooked in today's boardroom.

College presidents and trustees can create an ethical scorecard for themselves by asking eight questions. In their decision-making, they can check to see:

1. Is this something that ought to be changed?

2. Is this something we can affect?

3. Am I willing to pay the price for doing what is right?

4. Can I find a way to live with what cannot be changed?

5. Is it the truth?

6. Is it fair to all concerned?

7. Will it build goodwill and better friendships?

8. Will it be beneficial to all concerned?

If these questions are answered with care, trustees and presidents can proceed with the confidence that their decisions will pass the ethical test.

References

Boice, J. P. (2005, May). Minding the store: Are companies' corporate social responsibilities all they can be, or would businesses do better to concentrate on profits and losses? *Advancing Philanthropy,* 24–28.

Bolles, R. (2006). *What color is your parachute? 2007: A practical manual for job-hunters and career changes.* Berkeley, CA: Ten Speed Press.

Browning, T. (2005, June). The financial and ethics litmus test. *Executive Update,* 55–60.

Davis, G. (2000). Issues in community college governance. *New Expeditions Issues Papers*. Retrieved December 1, 2006, from www.aacc.nche .edu/Content/NavigationMenu/ResourceCenter/Projects_Partnerships /Current/NewExpeditions/IssuePapers/Issues_in_CC_Governance.htm

Hammonds, K. H. (2004, July). We incorporated. *Fast Company, 84,* 67–69.

Kerr, C. (1989). *The guardians: Boards of trustees of American colleges and universities: What they do and how well they do it.* Washington, DC: Association of Governing Boards of Universities and Colleges.

Kerr, C., & Gade, M. L. (1986). *The many lives of academic presidents: Time, place, and character.* Washington, DC: Association of Governing Boards of Universities and Colleges.

14

The Consequences of Compromised Ethical Identity Development in Community College Leadership

Clifford P. Harbour, Sharon K. Anderson, Timothy Gray Davies

In Chapter 6, "Professional Ethical Identity Development and Community College Leadership," we explained how community college leaders are encountering challenges that require a well-developed professional ethical identity. These challenges emerge from political, economic, and technological conditions. We argued that when leaders are faced with such challenges, a competent and moral resolution requires a well-developed professional ethical identity. To help leaders meet these challenges, we proposed and explained an acculturation model to facilitate professional ethical identity development in community college leaders.

Our model incorporated insights from Berry (1980, 2003), Berry and Sam (1997), and Handelsman, Gottlieb, and Knapp (2005). Concurring with Handelsman et al., we maintained that professional ethical identity development is best promoted through a strategy of integration. In fact, Handelsman et al. state that "people who adopt an *integration strategy* retain important aspects of their heritage but they also adopt what their new culture has to offer" (p. 60). This strategy may be affirmed by providing community college leaders with learning activities that incorporate the literature on professional ethical identity development, self-assessment of existing values, student role-playing, and journey mapping. As we explained, graduate education programs, state and college professional development programs, and even short-term workshops would be well served using these practices.

Of course, promoting a successful integration strategy is contingent on recognizing and responding to acculturation strategies that do not promote ethical identity development. Leaders committed to developing a professional ethical identity, either for themselves or for others, must recognize how an integration strategy can be developed using these specific learning activities. Additionally, they must recognize how alternative acculturation strategies may emerge, even without intending it, when leaders fail to find harmony between the personal values acquired over a career and those they encounter in a new organizational culture. This disharmony may occur by rejecting either personal or organizational values. In some cases, as we will explain, individuals may reject both personal and organizational values when encountering ethical problems. In any event, we would say the leader's rejection of personal or organizational values is unjustified or unwarranted, especially given that consideration of such values is necessary in resolving an ethical dilemma.

In this chapter, we develop and analyze three vignettes in which leaders exhibit acculturation strategies reflecting disharmony between the values they developed as a part of their heritage and those endorsed in the new organizational culture. We follow Berry (1980, 2003) and Handelsman et al. (2005) in characterizing these deficient acculturation strategies as *separation,* which entails unjustified rejection of new cultural values, *assimilation,* or the unwarranted rejection of personal values, and *marginalization,* in which leaders unjustifiably reject past personal values as well as the new organizational values. We describe and discuss these vignettes based on our experience. After presenting and analyzing these cases, we outline the conditions of a community college leadership culture in which leaders are encouraged to maintain and *integrate* commitments to their personal ethics of origin and to the community college's organizational values.

To facilitate this discussion, we proceed in the following manner. We begin with a brief account of Berry's (1980, 2003) acculturation model and Handelsman et al.'s (2005) ethical identity professional development theory. Next, we present three vignettes, drawn from a hypothetical People's Community College, that describe acculturation strategies (separation, assimilation, and marginalization) impeding professional ethical identity development. We then build on our positive recommendations in Chapter 6 and discuss how community colleges support a culture committed to ethical identity development. Finally, we present future research suggestions.

Acculturation and Professional Ethical Identity Development _____

As we explained in Chapter 6, Berry and Sam (1997) assert that a psychological acculturation process occurs when individuals encounter a different culture. When individuals have this experience, they effectively make two decisions: First, they make a decision concerning adherence to their culture of origin, including its values, beliefs, and ways of knowing. Second, they make a decision concerning adaptation to the new culture and its values, beliefs, and ways of knowing. Practically speaking, these decisions occur simultaneously, and the result is that individuals adopt one of the four acculturation strategies: assimilation, separation, marginalization, or integration. These strategies are varying approaches to resolving discrepancies between existing personal values and new organizational values.

Handelsman et al. (2005) use the psychological acculturation concept to explain how new professionals such as psychologists adapt to a new organization or profession and its ethical culture. Following Berry and Sam (1997), Handelsman et al. explain how new psychologists might develop a constructive professional ethical identity using an integration strategy. They also explain how new professionals might be limited in developing this professional ethical identity if they adopt assimilation, separation, or marginalization strategies—that is, strategies that reflect an individual's failure to balance or harmonize personal and organizational values.

We explained how leaders adopting an *integration* strategy develop a constructive professional ethical identity because they retain important personal values while internalizing moral beliefs and practices the new organization endorses. Handelsman et al. (2005) note that although these individuals may experience conflicts between their personal ethics code and the values the new profession endorses, they will be aware of this tension and work to resolve differences in ways that respect both value sets. Our vignette describing Henrietta Higgins explained how a community college leader may follow an integration strategy when faced with a dilemma created by commitments to different personal and organizational values.

We now turn to an examination of the less effective acculturation strategies.

Vignettes_____

Introduction: People's Community College

We examine deficient acculturation strategies in developing a professional ethical identity by recalling, revising, and updating Birnbaum's fictional People's Community College in his book *How Colleges Work: The Cybernetics of Academic Organization and Leadership* (1988). The new People's Community College (PCC) retains its comprehensive mission, including curricula serving students' needs in adult education, developmental studies, career programs, and transfer programs. PCC remains committed to student access, student success, low cost, and community responsiveness. As Birnbaum notes, the relatively high dependency on state funding brings a bureaucratic hue to the organization, emphasizing rules, procedures, and efficiency.

The new PCC has qualities that, although present in 1988, were not always acknowledged outside community college education. For instance, PCC now has a more diverse student population, unequaled at most four-year colleges and universities (Cohen & Brawer, 2003). Indeed, for several years now, no ethnic group has constituted a majority of PCC's student population. PCC also serves a higher proportion of students traditionally underrepresented at senior institutions, including first-generation students, women, immigrants, and people of color. PCC has many fiscal challenges, including diminished state support, limited external funding, and a federal student aid policy that has failed to keep up with the direct and indirect costs of acquiring a postsecondary education. Finally, despite its budgetary limitations, more community employers are calling on PCC to provide distance learning, contract training, and new innovative instructional programs (e.g., emergency management, IT certifications, and holistic health programs) designed to meet emerging community needs.

Ethical and competent leadership at PCC requires acknowledging and respecting its ambitious educational commitments, multicultural community, chronic fiscal challenges, and demands for innovative instructional programs. Developing leadership requires an underlying leadership philosophy that can hold to 20th-century social welfare values while operating under the constraints of 21st-century marketized higher education.

Our contention is that leaders possessing a suitable integration strategy are the best prepared to encounter the ethical issues that arise in these circumstances. But, as we explain next, leaders may also adopt acculturation strategies precluding appropriate ethical identity development; therefore, they undermine their PCC leadership responsibilities.

The Business Leader Comes to Campus

Adam Smith was PCC's new dean of continuing education, and his first six months on campus rivaled the best of employment honeymoons. Smith moved quickly to hire a new associate dean for workforce development, concluding a search that had stalled twice over the preceding year. He improved significantly his unit's quarterly reporting process. Now, reports included important comparisons with peer and neighboring institutions. The production schedule for these reports was accelerated, thereby providing President Stephen Johnson with critical data several weeks before PCC's quarterly board meetings. Finally, Smith was already instilling a new sense of pride in the continuing education department's 11 directors, an administrative group that had previously concluded PCC was much more interested in the department's revenue stream than its people. In meetings across the campus, Smith attributed these positive developments to the department's new business philosophy: efficient and effective decision-making. He maintained the unit's positive changes reflected the application of lessons he had learned and practiced while a division leader at Global Enterprises, Inc., an international construction firm.

Nonetheless, no honeymoon lasts forever. Just as Smith's first anniversary at PCC was arriving, Sarah Lawrence, the vice president for academic services, suffered a mild heart attack and took an extended three-month leave for what her cardiologist promised would be a nearly complete recovery. Smith temporarily assumed some of Lawrence's duties, which included replacing Lawrence as the search committee chair for the college's new computer animation and graphic design (CAGD) program director.

The three CAGD program director finalists all had industry experience, and each trumpeted her accomplishments in final interviews. Two finalists, Mary Anne Jones and Marsha Coppola, were polished professionals and had extensive managerial experience with the nationally known DreamTech Company. The position, however, would be their first in higher education. The third candidate, Cynthia Pixel, was a CAGD program coordinator at Metropolitan Community College. Pixel's experience at a major computer animation firm had been brief, only two years.

Smith sat down with search committee members and argued that Jones and Coppola, although having less teaching experience, would be better choices given their more extensive and current private sector experience. The committee members politely listened to Smith but unanimously endorsed Pixel. Smith's reasoning had failed to move the group, and he concluded the meeting declining their recommendation and requesting that Johnson extend an offer to either Jones or Coppola.

Two weeks later Smith was discussing an academic services division personnel matter with President Johnson. As Smith rose to leave, Louise Rollins, the president's executive assistant, casually asked if the search committee had made a recommendation for the CAGD program director. In a brief, stand-up meeting, Smith outlined the situation to Johnson and Rollins. He stuck to his position that the decision should be made on the basis of industry experience, and on this score he argued that Pixel was the least qualified candidate. Rollins reported, however, that she understood committee members believed Pixel had the best overall blend of instructional and industry experience, a priority the search committee previously had agreed on when they drafted the new job description.

Johnson listened attentively and then expressed his desire to have a unanimous recommendation. Rollins nodded, acknowledging Johnson's longstanding practice of moving methodically in making appointments when clear and deep divisions surfaced. Smith noted the comment and paused a moment before exclaiming, "But we can't wait too long, or we'll lose all of them!" President Johnson eyed Smith and responded in his inscrutable, deadpan voice, "That's right," and then stepped back into his office.

Smith could have asked Rollins for her advice as they left the president's office, but he did not. Smith could have met with the search committee again, but declined to do this as well. Instead, Smith forwarded the employment materials to President Johnson and, in a brief one-paragraph memo, recommended Jones for the position. After asking Rollins to meet with the search committee and consult with Lawrence at home, Johnson extended an offer to Pixel, and she promptly accepted.

Smith's first annual performance review and evaluation meeting followed two weeks later, and Johnson acknowledged the new vice president's accomplishments. But he cautioned Smith to be mindful that the faculty role in their search processes was a cultural empowerment previously negotiated and implemented. Smith was surprised. He perceived this last statement as a rebuke and responded curtly that a more businesslike approach to personnel matters "would no doubt help to replace the college's obsolete academic culture."

Smith never had a second evaluation at PCC. Within six months, he became discouraged by what he regarded as the president's lack of support for his business approach to management and soon left PCC for a private sector opportunity.

▰ *Analysis: Smith's Reaction to New Cultural Values*

Adam Smith came to PCC with an accomplished private sector record where values of efficiency and effectiveness were not tempered by a culture committed to shared governance, shared values, and participative decision-making. If Smith had done his homework before joining PCC, he would have discerned the college's commitment to these values; then, he could have chosen to prepare himself for this cultural conflict. But since arriving on campus, he never took the time to discuss the community college's culture with his PCC peers, nor did he make an earnest effort to understand why the institution's strategic planning, budgeting, and employment processes incorporated this culture. From his perspective, the commitment to shared governance, shared values, and participative decision-making was an archaic principle that the increasing marketization of higher education programs and services would soon replace. Smith assumed PCC's culture inevitably was transitioning to one that more closely resembled the private sector organizations he had encountered.

This vignette describes how Smith's ethical identity development at PCC was undermined by his adherence to personal ethics incompatible with PCC's organizational ethics. Smith's strong commitment to his personal ethics and his rejection of PCC's cultural values reflect a separation strategy. While separation does not necessarily signify an absence of professional ethical identity, it does denote the leader's inability to moderate a commitment to personal ethical identity and the positive cultural values PCC espoused.

The President's Dilemma

President Johnson recently completed his 10th year as president at PCC. Although he is now accorded great respect on campus and in the community, his first two years were difficult. PCC's previous president, Raymond Rogers, retired after 26 years as the institution's chief executive officer. Rogers was a popular president, and his strong commitment to local industry made him well regarded in the business community. Johnson, just beginning his first presidency, worked very hard to measure up. In fact, looking back at those first years, he could probably say he worked too hard to accommodate local industry requests, perhaps because it was a traditional PCC organizational value. This early attempt to honor industry requests was reflected most clearly in his first year and his handling of a curriculum issue.

At one of his first Rotary meetings, Ralph Goodwin, the CEO of Executive Hotels, Inc. (EHI), approached Johnson to discuss a new training initiative for EHI. Goodwin and Johnson arranged to meet later that week to discuss Goodwin's proposal for a new noncredit, 20-hour banquet service program to include 200 EHI employees. Later that week when Goodwin met Johnson, he presented two reasons EHI was requesting a noncredit program for its employees. First, he argued, PCC could provide instruction without "worrying about faculty accreditation issues." Second, Goodwin acknowledged he was aware that PCC's usual banquet service program was a 40-hour course that would transfer as a three-credit course into the college's AAS hospitality services degree program. But, Goodwin said, EHI's tuition reimbursement program only applied to credit courses or noncredit programs of 40 hours or more. Thus, with a customized 20-hour banquet service class, Goodwin could require employees to obtain the credential as a condition for continuing employment without reimbursing costs. Johnson said he would consider the proposal and get back to Goodwin the next week.

Johnson found himself on the horns of a dilemma. If he proceeded with the banquet service program, PCC would realize significant revenue, he would gain an important ally, and he might garner early Chamber of Commerce support. On the other hand, if Johnson declined to establish the customized program, he envisioned his commitment to the business community, local needs, and perhaps even the comprehensive mission coming into question. But Johnson's gut check told him the merit of Goodwin's proposal was ambiguous at best. The program would offer employee training under conditions precluding student reimbursement or progress toward an academic credential. He knew he would be favoring one constituency (EHI) to the detriment of another (potential PCC students).

Johnson needed help resolving the dilemma. He asked PCC's long-time vice president for continuing education, Sheila Kendell, for her advice. Soon, Johnson was persuaded that when all factors were considered the initiative was worth pursuing, and PCC would be viewed as having met an important corporate client's needs. Accordingly, Johnson decided not to gather any more information and asked Kendell to initiate the program. Proudly, he called Goodwin and assured him EHI's needs would be met.

The banquet program was beginning three weeks later when Johnson received a telephone call. It was his newly appointed board chair, Linda Washington, a local physician and NAACP local chapter board member. When Washington inquired about a new banquet service program the college was purportedly starting, Johnson confirmed that he had expedited Goodwin's request and was pleased to respond to a major corporate citizen like EHI. Johnson knew something was amiss, however, when a long pause ensued.

"Tell me, Stephen," Washington slowly asked, "have you attended a banquet at EHI's facilities?"

Johnson paused and then admitted that he had not.

"Well," Washington continued, "when you do, you'll no doubt notice the vast majority of the waitstaff are African American and Latino, and most of the banquet guests tend to be white."

Johnson looked out his office's large window, and the afternoon sun faintly illuminated a curious reflection: a president with egg on his face. "I think I see where you're going," Johnson said. "I just approved a program that will be training people of color to wait on white people."

"More than that," Washington added, "the waitstaff are not being reimbursed for their time and costs, right?"

"That's right Linda," Johnson replied. "I guess I was thinking my predecessor would have jumped at the opportunity, and I know he was very good with the business community."

Linda paused again and said, "Well Stephen, you're right, but this is a new day, and we need to find a new way to meet the needs of all our communities."

"Agreed," Johnson replied. "My apology, Linda."

"Apology accepted."

■ *Analysis: Johnson's Subordination of Personal Ethics*

President Johnson's desire to measure up to his predecessor's reputation and acknowledge traditional organizational values such as service to local industry disappointed his board chair and ultimately himself. Johnson knew that Goodwin's request was motivated by a desire to secure training under circumstances that would save EHI money, but would also deny

EHI employees reimbursement and offer them no help progressing toward a degree. His desire to respond promptly to Goodwin's request and emulate his predecessor's reputation deterred him from conducting a more thorough inquiry. Johnson also ignored his gut response, prompted by his personal ethics, to question an organizational value that rationalized the inequitable treatment of PCC constituencies.

This vignette describes a leader's strong endorsement of specific organizational values and subordination of personal ethics. Berry (2003) and Handelsman et al. (2005) refer to this as *assimilation,* a strategy for acculturation in which individuals regard explicit organizational values as comprehensive, admitting little room for nuance and personal ethics. Again, this strategy does not necessarily denote an absence of ethical identity; it denotes the leader's inability to develop a professional ethical identity drawing on and evaluating the cultural values against or with personal ethics.

The Lost Leader (Personal and Cultural Anomie)

President Johnson hired Karen Bishop three years ago as the new firearms instructor for PCC's Basic Law Enforcement Academy. Bishop came to PCC after a 20-year career with the city police department, where she attained the rank of patrol division sergeant. By all accounts, she had been a model police officer. Last year, however, Bishop's life changed when Kurt Wilber retired as the academy program director. After a brief internal search, Bishop was appointed interim director to finish the year. Just as Bishop was settling into the new position, John Deniston, an academy instructor, filed an academic dismissal notice against an academy cadet, alleging she had failed her third test in the course. Although the state's rules for law enforcement training clearly indicated that dismissal was an option available to the academy program director, the academy faculty agreed dismissal was not automatically required. The student responded, speaking to a PCC counselor and then filing a grievance against Deniston and Bishop, accusing them of harassment.

Vice President Sarah Lawrence, Dean Julia Littrell, and Bishop met on a Friday afternoon to clarify the issues. Littrell outlined a number of options, and she and Lawrence turned to Bishop for her perspective.

"So Karen," Littrell began, "what's your take on this? How would you like to proceed? Or, I guess more specifically, how can we maintain our standing with the law enforcement agencies while respecting the student's rights and acknowledging our fundamental values of student success?"

Bishop knew the question was a difficult one, and she began by noting the training officers for the local police departments were "vigorously advocating" for the student's dismissal.

"But," Bishop continued, "Jacob Risner in student counseling is telling me that if we proceed with the dismissal, we must follow the Student Academic Code, not the state's law enforcement training rules, and that means we need to provide an opportunity for remediation."

Lawrence, Littrell, and Bishop discussed the matter for another hour without any resolution and then agreed to meet again the following Tuesday to receive Bishop's recommendation.

The three leaders met again as scheduled, and everyone seemed to be in relatively good spirits, given their challenge. After 10 minutes of light banter, Lawrence noticed that Bishop was struggling with something. She interrupted the conversation, looked directly at Bishop and asked, "Karen what is it?"

"I just don't know," Bishop said. She stood up and walked over to the conference room window. "I guess I need to come clean with you on a couple of things."

"Okay," said Littrell, "tell us."

"You know," Bishop began, "I came to PCC because I had completed my law enforcement career. But it's also true that I became very disillusioned with the police department's culture my last few years and was looking for an out. Today, if you pressed me, I'd have to say that most law enforcement agencies with which I was familiar were more hierarchical than they needed to be. So, although I understand why department training officers are pushing to dismiss this cadet, it's not clear to me that she should be kicked out."

"That's fine," responded Lawrence. "I take it then you're ready to proceed with some sort of remediation. Is that right?"

"I guess," said Bishop. "But, to be candid, is that really the best way to proceed?"

Littrell and Lawrence exchanged puzzled glances.

"What do you mean?" Littrell asked.

"Well," Karen replied, "why should we spend all this time with remediation? Won't that just be a waste of resources? The student had her chance just like everyone else, and she did fail three tests."

Littrell sat back in her chair and slowly pulled her yellow pad toward her.

"Wait a minute Karen," Littrell began, "I thought you said this cadet was a first-generation college student."

"Yes, that's true," Bishop acknowledged.

"And didn't you also say in your interview for the interim position that you were committed to student success even if this required supplemental instruction or remediation?"

"Sure," Karen responded. "So what?

"So what?" Lawrence exclaimed. "Don't we have an ethical obligation to help this student and provide remediation in these circumstances?"

"I don't know," Bishop responded. "You see, I'm not sure it will be worth the effort. My gut tells me the training officers are forcing this issue just to show the students how authority works in paramilitary organizations. I understand this and don't like it. But, I also have doubts that remediation is really going to make a difference with this cadet."

"But shouldn't we try it first before coming to conclusions?" Lawrence asked.

"I just don't know," Bishop replied. "To be honest, I just don't know."

Analysis: Marginalization and Leadership Paralysis

Bishop struggled to deal with the academic grievance against the cadet in light of relevant cultural and personal values. After 20 years in law enforcement, Bishop had lost her faith in the hierarchical, paramilitary law enforcement culture. Furthermore, she had not yet internalized critical PCC organizational values such as student success and student access. The consequence was that Bishop was alienated from both her former law enforcement culture and the organizational culture of PCC. She was effectively paralyzed.

Berry (2003) and Handelsman et al. (2005) refer to this strategy as *marginalization,* a behavior pattern where individuals have low identification with both previous personal ethics and new organization values. Like other strategies, marginalization does not necessarily denote an ethical identity absence; it denotes rather the leader's inability to develop a professional ethical identity drawing from both professional cultural values and personal ethics.

Community College Cultures Supporting Ethical Identity Development: Promoting an Integration Strategy During the Acculturation Journey _____

Our discussion has demonstrated how community college leaders may adopt deficient acculturation strategies when attempting to resolve the tension between personal ethics and new community college cultural values. Handelsman et al. (2005) indicate these adverse acculturation strategies may be temporary, exhibited in explicit or implicit behaviors, and resolved in a variety of ways. Our objective now is to outline the conditions of a community college leadership culture in which individuals are encouraged to maintain and integrate commitments to their personal ethics of origin and to the community college's organizational values.

We contend a culture that successfully supports its leaders as they develop a professional ethical identity must be positive and constructive, and this development process must be regarded as a long-term project. When professional ethical identity development is grounded in such assumptions, community college leaders will gradually develop the trust and commitment needed to construct and utilize integration strategies. We now outline three conditions of such a culture.

Articulation of Community College Organizational Values

First, we believe most community college practitioners will recall instances where developing leaders retained an unwarranted commitment to values developed earlier in their careers or through prior life experiences. The vignette describing Adam Smith's travails reflected the challenges institutions face when leaders retain such personal values and are unable to internalize new organizational values. Our experience tells us that an essential first step in promoting commitment to critical organizational values is articulating these values clearly at places and times deemed important by the institution's culture. Often we assume that new leaders understand such principles as the comprehensive mission, the open-door admissions policy, and student success. Invariably, however, some new employees do not get the message, and this is especially problematic when they have leadership responsibilities.

Accordingly, when appropriate, we advocate articulating and explaining community college organizational values during critical events and celebrations (e.g., graduation, new employee orientations, and employee retirement celebrations). These activities are conducted routinely with a view toward important organizational values, but leaders often forget to emphasize their relevance. We suggest that community college leaders promote these values more explicitly. Purposefully articulating organizational values does not need to lead to a culture of slogans or buzzwords. However, when appropriate and in circumstances that preserve the values' integrity and the institution's dignity, we contend articulation is not only appropriate, but also necessary. Such actions would help all college community members understand the organizational values to be incorporated; they would also help future leaders integrate their personal ethics with the organization's ethics and values.

Awareness of and Respect for Personal Ethics of Origin

Community college cultures committed to professional ethical identity development must meet a second condition: a genuine awareness of and respect for personal ethics. President Johnson revealed how a new leader inadvertently may act in a manner that misapplies organizational values. This vignette also demonstrated how a leader might compromise his or her personal ethics and personal integrity as a result. President Johnson's specific error was failing to consider the limitations or boundaries of a specific organizational value associated with a successful predecessor.

A genuine awareness of and respect for personal ethics should not be difficult to embrace, given the long-standing community college commitment to diversity. Now, however, diversity must go beyond inclusion of different people to inclusion of different personal ethics. We are not calling on institutions to accept leadership guided by personal codes of ethics based on intolerance or abuse or disrespect of others. We do, however, contend that community colleges must be willing to accept personal ethics developed in other organizational settings such as communities of faith, the business community, other higher education cultures, or the military. Personal codes of ethics developed by leaders through experience in other professions should be regarded as a means to enhance the richness and meaning of the community college's traditional values. Achieving this end will require greater efforts to curtail the us-versus-them mentality often used to distinguish community colleges from other organizational settings. Perhaps most importantly, campuses should be explicit in affirming their respect for different personal ethics.

Successful Institutional Integration of Organizational Values and Personal Ethics

Finally, we believe a third condition needed to support a community college culture committed to professional ethical identity development is integration of differing personal ethics and the organization's values at the institutional level. Campus leaders must not only articulate the organization's values and demonstrate a genuine awareness of and respect for personal ethics, but they also must promote participation in learning activities that will enable campus leaders to understand professional ethical identity development and the effective and ineffective acculturation strategies discussed earlier. As we explained in Chapter 6, these learning activities may be incorporated into graduate leadership programs, state leadership development academies, and campus professional development programs. They should all include discussion of the literature on professional ethical identity development, self-assessment of existing personal values, student role play using problems and issues relevant to the institution, and journey mapping to help leaders monitor the evolution of their professional ethical identity.

These efforts will only succeed, however, if professional ethical identity becomes an aspect of how we assess and develop campus leaders. This does not mean leadership development should discount acquisition of other skills and knowledge; it does mean that when relevant issues arise (as demonstrated in the vignettes) the integration of personal ethics and organizational values should be a matter of discussion when leaders are assessed on performance.

Conclusion

This discussion has followed our remarks in Chapter 6, "Professional Ethical Identity Development and Community College Leadership," and focused specifically on acculturation strategies reflecting a deficiency in balancing or harmonizing personal ethics and organizational values. These strategies were explained through vignettes revealing how leaders might falter in developing their professional ethical identity. In our previous chapter, we described the components of learning activities that could be used to develop an individual's professional ethical identity. In this chapter, we explained how professional ethical identity development can be promoted at the institutional level. This may be accomplished by supporting an institutional culture that articulates fundamental community college values, respects personal ethics, and prioritizes the integration of organizational values and personal ethics.

Of course, we recognize that our work only represents the first steps in acquiring a greater understanding of professional ethical identity development at the community college. A more complete knowledge of these issues will follow from community college research. Qualitative researchers would add to our knowledge by examining the experiences and stories of individuals on the path toward constructive professional ethical identity development. Quantitative researchers would contribute to our knowledge base by soliciting leaders' perceptions of how they reconcile personal ethics and organizational values.

References

Berry, J. W. (1980). Acculturation as varieties of adaptation. In A. M. Padilla (Ed.), *Acculturation: Theory, models, and some new findings* (pp. 9–25). Boulder, CO: Westview Press.

Berry, J. W. (2003). Conceptual approaches to acculturation. In K. M. Chun, P. B. Organista, & G. Marin (Eds.), *Acculturation: Advances in theory, measurement, and applied research* (pp. 17–37). Washington, DC: American Psychological Association.

Berry, J. W., & Sam, D. L. (1997). Acculturation and adaptation. In J. W. Berry, M. H. Segall, & C. Kagitcibasi (Eds.), *Handbook of cross-cultural psychology: Vol. 3. Social behaviour and applications* (2nd ed., pp. 291–326). Boston, MA: Allyn & Bacon.

Birnbaum, R. (1988). *How colleges work: The cybernetics of academic organization and leadership.* San Francisco, CA: Jossey Bass.

Cohen, A. M., & Brawer, F. B. (2003). *The American community college* (4th ed.). San Francisco, CA: Jossey-Bass.

Handelsman, M. M., Gottlieb, M. C., & Knapp, S. (2005, February). Training ethical psychologists: An acculturation model. *Professional Psychology: Research and Practice, 36*(1), 59–65.

Index

absolutism, xii, 77, 105
accountability, 25, 26, 62, 75, 81
acculturation, 62, 63, 65, 71, 73, 75, 166, 167, 168, 169, 175, 178, 180, 181
administrator(s). *See* staff
Allegory of the Cave, 19
altruism, 35, 37, 42, 43
American Association of Community Colleges, viii, ix, 38, 45, 115, 120, 133, 156
American Association of University Administrators, 115, 120
American College Personnel Association, 115
Amey, M. J., 61, 74, 132, 143, 144
Anderson, P., 74
Anderson, S. K., 61, 63, 74, 77, 166
Anding, J. M., 87
Andrews, K. R., 122, 130
Aristotle, 3, 4, 6, 10, 14, 34, 78
assessment, 32, 62, 70, 72, 73, 82, 166, 180
assimilation, 63, 64, 167, 168, 175
Association of College and University Professors, 115
Association of Institutional Researchers, 115
Astin, A. W., 146, 153
Astin, H. S., 146, 153
authenticity, 89, 98, 100

Bachrach, P., 26, 31

Baker, G. A., 61, 75
Baratz, M. S., 26, 31
Bass, B. M., 14
Bassoppo-Mayo, S., 76
behaviorist theories, 8
Bell, C. S., 132, 143
Berg, E., 24, 31
Berry, J. W., 62, 63, 64, 65, 71, 73, 75, 166, 167, 168, 172, 175, 177, 181
Birnbaum, R., 169, 181
Blaisdell, B., 6, 14
board members, 38, 42, 47, 50, 55, 56, 57, 155, 156
Boice, J. P., 155, 163, 164
Bolden, R., 8, 9, 11, 14
Bolles, R., 159, 164
Brady, F. N., 104, 121
Brawer, F. B., 169, 181
Bretz, R. D., 128, 130
Brown, L., 61, 74, 75
Brown, T. M., 143
Browning, T., 155, 164
Buddemeier, S., 132, 143
Buddhism, 5
Burns, J. M., 9, 14, 44, 45

CAO, 93, 99
Caplan, R. D., 128, 130
categorical imperative, 35, 37, 42
Christian virtues, 6
Cleary, T., 7, 8, 14
Cohen, A. M., 169, 181

communitarianism, 35, 37, 42
Confucius, 4, 5, 8, 14
Cooper, J. E., 132, 143
Covey, S. R., 9, 13, 14
Crittenden, L., 61, 75
cultural capital, 27
cultural norms, xi, 23, 25, 27, 31
culture, 2, 5, 6, 7, 25, 26, 27, 31,
    43, 44, 51, 53, 63, 64, 66, 70,
    79, 141, 143, 166, 167, 168,
    171, 172, 176, 177, 178, 179,
    180, 181
curriculum, 30, 45, 71, 89, 92, 93,
    94, 95, 97, 137, 150, 173

Daniel, D., 61, 75
Davies, T. G., 61, 74, 75, 77, 166, 181
Davis, G., 156, 165
Davis, J. R., 34, 41, 45
Davis, M., 61, 75
deans. *See* staff
Deitemeyer, K., 132, 143
democratic constitution, 20
DePree, M., 80, 81, 86
Devanna, M. A., 9, 15
Dewey, J., 34, 45
DiCroce, D., 132, 143
directors. *See* staff
dissonance, 90, 96, 97, 98, 99, 101,
    102, 104
Downing, S., 79, 83, 84, 86

Ecclestone, K., 27, 32
empirical studies, 61
Enron, 39
ethical identity development,
    xi, 62, 63, 64, 65, 66, 70, 71,
    74, 166, 167, 170, 172, 178,
    179, 180, 181

ethical pluralism, 35, 37
ethical principles, ix, 16, 17, 90,
    101, 116
ethical sphere, 28
ethics, vii, viii, xiii, 3, 5, 7, 8, 10,
    11, 12, 13, 14, 21, 22, 28, 33,
    34, 37, 38, 39, 40, 41, 42, 44,
    45, 47, 54, 58, 59, 62, 64, 65,
    70, 72, 74, 76, 88, 89, 90, 96,
    98, 99, 100, 101, 104, 105,
    107, 108, 112, 114, 115, 116,
    117, 118, 119, 120, 121, 123,
    150, 154, 155, 157, 164, 167,
    168, 172, 175, 177, 178, 179,
    180, 181
Exley, R., 34, 45

faculty, x, xi, xii, 3, 11, 12, 13, 14,
    23, 24, 25, 26, 27, 28, 29, 30,
    31, 37, 38, 41, 42, 43, 47, 49,
    50, 52, 53, 62, 66, 67, 69, 76,
    80, 81, 82, 83, 86, 89, 92, 93,
    94, 95, 96, 97, 100, 103, 105,
    107, 108, 109, 110, 113, 115,
    116, 117, 119, 125, 127, 132,
    137, 138, 139, 140, 145, 147,
    148, 149, 150, 151, 152, 154,
    156, 171, 173, 175
fairness, vii, xi, 33, 35, 36, 37, 39,
    42, 43, 86, 89, 119, 134, 141,
    142, 161
feminist care ethics, 3
Festinger, L., 98, 102
Fletcher, J. F., 118, 121
Folkman, J., 28, 29, 32
Four-Way Test, viii, ix, 160, 161,
    162, 163

Gade, M. L., 160, 165

Giannini, S. T., 133, 144
Golden Rule, 28, 86
Gottlieb, M. C., 62, 75, 166, 181
governing boards, 42
great man theory, 8
Greenleaf, R. K., 114, 121

Hammonds, K. H., 163, 165
Handelsman, M. M., 62, 63, 64, 65,
71, 73, 74, 75, 166, 167, 168,
172, 175, 177, 178, 181
Harbour, C., 62, 75
Hardy, D. E., 116, 117, 121
Hersh, R. H., 79, 86
Hesselbein, F., 16, 21, 22
honesty, 41, 42, 43, 79, 89, 94, 99,
116, 128, 134, 141
Hurricane Katrina, 58

idealized attributes, 11
individualized consideration, 10
influence, vii, viii, 6, 8, 23, 24, 25,
26, 27, 29, 31, 32, 42, 63, 86
inspirational motivation, 10
integration strategy, xiii, 62, 65,
66, 67, 70, 71, 72, 74, 166,
168, 169
intellectual stimulation, 10

Johnson, C. E., 34, 36, 37, 45
journaling, 73
Judge, T. A., 128, 130
justice, vii, xii, 3, 16, 17, 35, 36, 37,
42, 43, 53, 59, 86, 118, 119

Kane, K., 28, 29, 31, 32
Kant, I., 28, 35
Kerr, C., 154, 159, 160, 165
Kies, D., 79, 86

Knapp, S., 62, 75, 166, 181
Kouzes, J. M., 81, 82, 87, 133,
134, 144

Lama, D., 28, 29, 31, 32, 79, 87
Lawton, A., 11, 14
leaders(s), vii, viii, ix, x, xi, xii, 7, 8,
9, 10, 11, 13, 17, 18, 19, 20, 21,
22, 25, 28, 32, 33, 36, 37, 39,
40, 41, 43, 44, 48, 59, 61, 62,
63, 66, 70, 71, 72, 73, 74, 75,
80, 81, 86, 103, 104, 108, 109,
111, 112, 114, 116, 117, 119,
120, 123, 124, 126, 127, 129,
130, 131, 132, 133, 134, 135,
142, 144, 146, 147, 148, 150,
151, 152, 155, 160, 161, 162,
166, 167, 168, 169, 176, 178,
179, 180, 181
leadership, vii, viii, ix, x, xi, xii, 1, 2,
7, 8, 9, 11, 16, 20, 32, 33, 38,
42, 45, 61, 74, 77, 78, 80, 81,
103, 123, 131, 132, 133, 144,
145, 146, 151, 153, 166, 168,
169, 177, 180, 181
leadership development, 28, 61,
62, 147, 148, 149, 150, 151,
152, 180
learner-centered instruction, 82
learning facilitators, 71
Lovaglia, M. J., 24, 32
Lovell, N., 61, 75
loyalty, 55, 56, 79, 128, 155

Macaulay, M., 11, 14
MacDowell, M. A., 58, 60
marginalization, 63, 65, 167,
168, 177
Markovsky, B., 24, 32

Martinez, M., 61, 75
McArthur, R. C., 61, 76
McGonigal, K., 81, 87
McGregor, D., 14
mentoring, 43, 109
Miller, M. T., 61, 76
mission, viii, x, xi, 10, 12, 13, 16,
    18, 19, 20, 21, 22, 23, 25, 26,
    30, 31, 51, 62, 66, 67, 68, 70,
    90, 98, 115, 120, 123, 124, 125,
    128, 129, 148, 149, 150, 169,
    173, 178
Moore, G. K., 63, 74, 132
morality, 2, 3, 5, 34, 50, 112, 118,
    121, 133, 154
Murray, J. P., 61, 74
myths, 2, 39

Nagy, P., 62, 75
National Association of Student
    Financial Aid Administrators,
    115, 121
New Testament, 6
Niebuhr, R., 59, 60, 157
Northern Africa, 6
Northouse, P. G., 33, 34, 42, 43,
    44, 45

obedience, 54, 55
Old Testament, 6
oligarchic constitution, 20
Olivarez, A., Jr., 61, 74

Palmer, P. J., 79, 87
personal value system, 63
Phi Theta Kappa, 16
philosophers, 18, 157
Plato, xi, 1, 3, 8, 10, 16, 21, 22, 34,
    99, 102, 155

Pope, M. L., 61, 76
positional authority, 39
Posner, B. Z., 81, 82, 87, 133,
    134, 144
power, xi, 5, 11, 21, 23, 24, 25, 26,
    27, 29, 31, 44, 50, 82, 90, 108,
    121, 143, 155, 160
president(s), vii, x, xi, xii, 23, 24, 25,
    26, 27, 30, 31, 33, 34, 35, 36,
    37, 38, 39, 40, 41, 42, 43, 44,
    46, 47, 48, 49, 50, 51, 52, 53,
    54, 55, 56, 57, 58, 59, 74, 93,
    97, 103, 105, 106, 109, 110,
    112, 124, 132, 133, 134, 135,
    136, 137, 138, 139, 140, 141,
    142, 143, 144, 146, 147, 148,
    149, 150, 152, 154, 155, 156,
    157, 158, 159, 161, 162, 164,
    172, 174

Qur'ān, 2, 6
Quick, D., 61, 75
Quinn, R. E., 82, 83, 87

Rachels, J., 3, 14, 34, 45
Rachman, S., 99, 100, 102
Rawls, J., 36
respect, xiii, 5, 6, 11, 26, 37, 38, 42,
    44, 57, 66, 74, 79, 81, 82, 85,
    89, 90, 97, 116, 129, 134, 150,
    163, 172, 179, 180
Richardson, B., 77, 78, 82, 87
Rivers, T. M., 79, 80, 87
Rogers, C., 89, 102, 172, 174
Rosenberg, D., 2, 15

Safty, A., 151, 152, 153
Sam, D. L., 62, 63, 64, 65, 73, 75,
    166, 168, 181

Schneider, C. G., 79, 86
separation, 63, 64, 100, 167, 168, 172
servant leadership, 30, 114
Shanks, T., 85, 86, 87
Shapiro, J. P., 40, 45
shared vision, 82
Shults, C., 132, 144
Siegel, B. L., 80, 82, 87
staff, x, xii, 12, 23, 24, 25, 28, 29, 30, 37, 38, 39, 43, 49, 50, 56, 68, 69, 92, 93, 107, 111, 113, 115, 117, 119, 124, 138, 145, 146, 147, 149, 151, 152, 174
Starratt, R. J., 122, 130
Stefkovich, J. A., 40, 45
Stephenson, G. W., 132, 144
Stern, G. G., 128, 130
Stillion, J. M., 80, 82, 87
Stout-Stewart, S., 131, 134, 144
students, x, xii, 12, 16, 23, 25, 26, 29, 30, 35, 37, 38, 41, 42, 49, 50, 51, 52, 53, 54, 55, 56, 58, 62, 67, 68, 69, 78, 80, 81, 83, 85, 86, 89, 90, 91, 92, 93, 94, 95, 96, 97, 98, 100, 103, 105, 107, 108, 110, 112, 113, 115, 119, 124, 125, 127, 128, 134, 135, 136, 137, 138, 140, 141, 142, 145, 146, 147, 148, 149, 150, 151, 152, 154, 155, 156, 157, 158, 161, 162, 169, 173, 177
Stumpf, D., 75

Taoism, 4, 5
Tedrow, B., 132, 144
Terry, R. W., 100, 102

theory, 3, 5, 7, 8, 10, 11, 12, 13, 14, 26, 34, 44, 71, 72, 75, 91, 102, 119, 130, 134, 135, 142, 167, 181
Tichy, N. M., 9, 15
Tillich, P., 100, 101, 102
timocratic constitution, 20
Townsend, B. K., 61, 76, 143
transformation theories, 9
transformational leadership, 9, 11, 12, 13, 133, 134
trustees, viii, x, xi, xiii, 25, 46, 47, 48, 49, 50, 51, 53, 54, 55, 56, 57, 59, 61, 74, 106, 108, 135, 141, 154, 155, 156, 157, 158, 159, 161, 164
truth, 6, 160
Twombly, S. B., 132, 144
tyranny, 21
Tzu, L., 7, 15, 81

unethical behavior, 31, 49, 58, 104, 114, 155, 156
universal responsibility, 29, 79
utilitarianism, 35, 37, 40, 42

values, viii, xi, xiii, 10, 13, 16, 17, 18, 19, 21, 22, 25, 26, 32, 34, 37, 38, 39, 40, 41, 51, 52, 53, 62, 63, 64, 65, 66, 67, 70, 71, 72, 73, 74, 79, 88, 97, 98, 128, 154, 156, 158, 159, 160, 166, 167, 168, 169, 172, 174, 175, 177, 178, 179, 180, 181
VanDerLinden, K. E., 61, 74
Van Harrison, R., 130
Vaughan, G. B., 33, 39, 45, 61, 76, 132, 133, 144
vice president(s). *See* staff

virtue, x, 2, 3, 4, 5, 6, 7, 8, 11, 12,
    13, 14, 19, 20, 104, 141
virtue theory, 3, 7, 8, 13

Waggoner, H. T., 63, 74
Wattenbarger, J. C., 27
Weingartner, R. H., 115, 121

Weisman, I. M., 132, 144
Wheatley, M. J., 26, 32
Willer, D., 24, 32
wisdom, 6, 11, 17, 81, 157, 160, 161
Wise-Choice Process, 84, 85

Zenger, J. H., 28, 29, 32